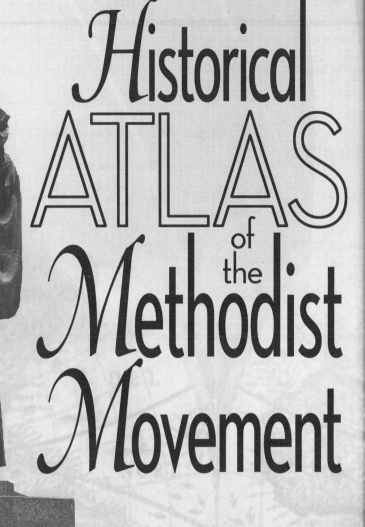

Historical ATLAS of the Methodist Movement

W. HARRISON DANIEL

Abingdon Press
NASHVILLE

Historical Atlas of the Methodist Movement

Copyright © 2009 by Abingdon Press

This book is printed on acid-free paper.

Library of Congress Cataloging-in-Publication Data

Daniel, William Harrison.
 Historical atlas of the Methodist movement / William Harrison Daniel.
  p. cm.
 ISBN 978-0-687-65651-6 (binding: printed book with cd/dvd insert, pbk., adhesive : alk. paper)
 1. Methodist Church--History--Maps. I. Title.

 G1046.E423D3 2009
 287.022'3--dc22

2008049698

09 10 11 12 13 14 15 16 17 18—10 9 8 7 6 5 4 3 2 1

MANUFACTURED IN THE UNITED STATES OF AMERICA

Contents

Locations and Legacies

A Historical Atlas of the Methodist Family

Why should maps matter to Methodists? Why should Methodists and the wider Wesleyan family care about a historical atlas? The People Called Methodists and their progeny have always been a curiously restless people. John Wesley's earliest historical account of Methodism described the movement in geographic terms as the "Three Rises of Methodism." Before it was ever a church, Methodism in Britain and the American colonies was a religious movement that practiced its theological convictions across vast distances. According to Wesley, the story of the movement turned on geographic reference points. The trans-Atlantic Wesleyan revival was first located spatially among the dreaming spires of Oxford, England; then in Wesley's dreams of mission among the unspoiled natives of Georgia; and after picking up the pieces of a failed mission and love interest, Wesley's search for spiritual assurance lead him back to London's Aldersgate Street. Clearly, Wesley's earliest historical narrative is already a type of atlas, finding narrative meaning as the movement spread geographically. Thus, history for Methodists has been inseparable from spatial movement. Even once the British and American churches were established, they were rarely static. Rather, the Wesleyan traditions have continually been a family of churches "on the move." Like other vital religious movements, Methodism and its various cousins began in concrete places, and then quickly traveled. Methodism has moved and grown in certain theological, sociological, and geographical directions toward purposes that met the needs of particular places and times. As a result, maps are critical to interpret Methodism in all its worldwide forms and reforms.

Questions requiring a historical atlas still abound. Indeed, as a faith group, if you want to know were you came from, where you are, and where you are going, maps are handy companions. Methodism and its related movements have needed answers precisely to these kinds of questions—for almost three hundred years. Other questions must be posed by each new generation of Wesleyan leaders: where are we in relation to the Church of England, from which Methodists emerged as a renewal movement? The very name *Church of England* indicates a church rooted very deeply in a time and a space. How did Methodism relate itself to that church and then root itself and reach outward to eighteenth-century Britain? How did Methodists preach throughout Britain, becoming an independent church? Where are American Methodists and related movements today, and how did we arrive at our particular places, times, and with our unique characteristics? A theological movement that sees the need for Christians to "go on to perfection"; to spread scriptural holiness; to renew the nation beginning with the churches—operates in unique ways: it sees its mission statement as a group moving together through space and time in very intentional patterns. A church with these theological presuppositions needs maps—to know where in the world is their parish.

Yet where in the world was Methodism's parish? How did it diffuse, especially across the evolving American landscape? Narratives from earlier periods often emphasized that Methodism grew because its circuit riders were highly frontier adaptive. Our historical atlas reveals a somewhat more nuanced story, depending on region and era. For the American scene, Methodism and other Wesleyan movements acted in great stretch initiatives, but quickly followed up with ethical, activist, institutional building. This restless people possessed theological impulses to move into the world, in order to remove "the world" from God's spaces and reveal the presence of God at work in this new nation. Both the means and the ends of these movements left a curious "footprint" on American space. Before Methodism reached the entire Mississippi river basin by the 1830s—that symbolic center of the country—itinerant preachers were successfully adapting to rapidly growing agrarian settlements as much as to the frontier.

Indeed, no sooner had Methodism reached the new frontiers chasing westward demographic movements than the frontier grew into settlements, and Methodism consequently grew with it. That Methodism was at home in the growing agrarian settlements stretching west from the Middle Atlantic States, and then towards the South, can be seen in our maps that follow. One need only look at the names of the earliest circuits on our maps to see this point: the vast majority of the time, the names of the earliest "frontier" circuits were actually places where rivers, roads, and consequently settlements were rapidly converging and developing.

Maps help us see how our Wesleyan family left their footprints across this land. We are a faith tradition that sees God already at work over the next hill. So we scatter preachers to go out into the corners of any landscape or nation. Yet we also believe that Wesleyans should gather together at regular intervals to renew ourselves in the grace of God. Through small groups and institutions, we historically have connected to each other in particular places to "go on to perfection" in love. Our theology is often expressed in a spatial journey that begins where we are in prevenient grace, orients us to God in justifying grace, and then calls us "move on" toward individual and social renewal in sanctifying grace. Our history across space and time clearly demonstrates that any theology of grace can and should be found present in shared sacred spaces and practices. To this end, our maps demonstrate where and why many of these sacred nurturing institutions have been placed. The atlas depicts both a scattered and gathered people—a people that moved, and movements that established graced people, places, and institutions.

Maps are also important to our Wesleyan family because of our shared theology. Because we claim Christ died for the entire world (and not just the "elect" of our own people), our movements through the world take on deep spiritual and sacramental meanings. As Wesleyans, we continue to express the journey of sanctification in concrete space and time, toward the very horizons of the earth and its cultures. We also need to mark the places where God's grace and our human response have intersected. Sacred places on a map, after all, simply represent the coming together of persons and practices, guided as much by an internal moral compass as any magnetic compass. The sacred places of our traditions depicted in this atlas point theologically to the ever-evolving connections between the Wesleyan movement, our neighbors, and our nation. This task reminds us of Abraham's journey from his home in Ur to the promised land of Palestine. While we do not know if he had a map, we do know he marked the places where he worshiped God with altars he made among other peoples along the journey. A Wesleyan historical atlas should matter for the same reason: to mark the places and the paths where we have found worship with God among people as we move ever closer to the full promises of God's New Creation. We need good maps to mark the spot for clues where a community of faith meets a God reconciling the whole world in Christ.

But can maps truly help us on *spiritual* journeys? I believe they can, if we strictly define their use and limitations. Whatever else they are, maps themselves reflect the space and time of their production, as much as the places they depict. Yet ironically, as a product of space and time, they do not fully capture either. For no map lasts forever, and no time can ever be fully placed. There is something of a mysterious coming together of persons and places in time that can never be represented in the frozen snapshot of a map. Yet we need them. Indeed, if you want to locate that new Sushi restaurant, if you want to discover where your instant messaging "pen pal" lives, or if you wish to find an exciting new destination for your next Sunday drive, then for all of these important decisions and more you surely need a map. Maps, in a truly profound sense, help us find each other and our place in the world each day. In the process, maps help us find ourselves along the way.

As a human product, however, maps are clearly limited. Maps—particularly historical atlases—must condense and represent vast amounts of historical, geographical, cultural, and demographic data, all in some sense of order, while depicting changes in those variables. Historical geographers are forced to select, like all historians, from the available sources and then to tell a good story, as partial as all historical and geographical stories are. Yet, even within literature, we know that a good story, and how its characters act within the story, needs a well-developed (but not exhaustive) treatment of the setting. Getting the setting right, according to Hemingway, is crucial to establishing how characters move and interact. Without a well-developed setting, character and plot cannot find resolution in any realistic and "moving" conclusion. In this sense, the selections made and depicted in any map are attempts to describe the settings through which Methodists and other Wesleyans moved and connected with people in the world around them.

The problem of selection in maps was in the news a few years ago. The state of Georgia updated its official state map, and tough choices faced the cartographers. Many towns in rural areas had practically ceased to have any population. And when the mapmakers omitted these places, there was considerable protest from persons in the region, not to mention from family members whose ancestors had lived and died in these small towns. To omit places from the map was to erase family histories and regional identities, and to let the sands of time completely wash over communities, simply because they were no longer economically viable. Many of the place names were included in a supplement, and the State of Georgia marches on to the beat of the New South. But it was clear from this event that maps both place and erase people's journeys and identities. The mapmaker's task, like the teacher's, should not be entered into lightly. For when we map people, places, and things, we have the power to both create and destroy.

Beyond the problems of selection and limitations of sources, lies another challenge. There is a clear problem in rendering spiritual realities spatially. Our notions of what constitutes true religious expression will certainly have an impact on how we draw our maps. Each of us reads a historical atlas of religion with an implicit theology of geography and carto-graphy. A map can teach us what these implicit theologies are through what irritates us in a map; by what angers us in omissions; and by the relative weight we assign to the interrelationships between persons of faith, institutions, and the environments through which they move and develop. Some important events happen in any religious history that we will never know about, or which must remain invisible and inaudible. The preaching and particularly the prayers of circuit riders come to mind here. And if we are blind to some invisible realities, perhaps we have focused on certain events and places disproportionately. Persons or groups that moved across landscapes in great "stretch initiatives" or made large institutional contributions to a place or a region have probably been overly represented due to spatial demands. We will leave such issues for other historians to critique. Yet I harbor hope that perhaps even the limitations of our map will spark interest in others to make their own maps. This is necessary, because all maps—as selections—become distortions. And distortions are corrected only through the complement of many different kinds of maps. From Mercator to various Azimuth projections, to the atlases of the southern continents that counter northern arrogance by "inverting" the map—there are perspective choices to be made in maps. These choices should prompt us to approach the historical data from different angles in the future and to inspire new religious mapmakers to complement our work.

The challenge of a historical atlas is the challenge of writing and producing any good novel or film: how to place the right characters together in the right places, at the right times, to simulate reality, and hopefully to stimulate response in the audience. Where this atlas has not achieved this goal, I bear the sole responsibility. Yet I am cheered in my attempts by the many friends and guides who have helped me to see this exciting Wesleyan story in clearer historical and spatial terms. I am deeply grateful for the assistance of some of the best interpreters of United Methodist history in America: Rex Matthews, Tom Frank, Russell Richey, Wesley de Souza, Darryl Stephens, Stephen Gunter, Dana Robert, Bishop Bevel Jones, Bishop Woodie White, and Darrell Whiteman.

I wish to especially thank Professor Andrew Walls—Scottish Methodist and patient mentor. He has been a trusted guide to me and my family for many journeys and many years.

All of these persons have informed the atlas on every page (perhaps in ways they would not recognize or authorize!).

This historical atlas is designed to illustrate and illuminate the fine texts of Rex Matthews (*Timelines of Methodist History*) and Russell Richey (*Methodist Experience in America*, vols. I and II, with Rowe and Schmidt). To plot a historical event, one needs to locate it in a social space and time. Few other commentators of Methodism have done a better job of placing the tradition in its time coordinates than Matthews and Richey. I hope that my historical atlas and accompanying CD-ROM (*A Historical Atlas of World Methodism powered by Google Earth*) will locate Wesleyan movements in ways that coordinate and complement their work. It is an honor to play the role of space to their time. The limitations of my text, maps, and the connections to their rich texts, however, clearly remain with me.

In the end, there are some things in the heart and soul of any spiritual wanderer that cannot be mapped. Much of any spiritual journey, for the individual as well as for a religious movement, must remain a mystery. In connection with this, I wish to thank my editor, Dr. Robert Ratcliff of The United Methodist Publishing House. He has been an instrument of editorial grace and inspiration—a trusted counselor on what should and should not be mapped in a historical atlas of religion. If there is a measure of grace in these maps, it is surely a testimony to his vision and guidance on this creative new project.

The novelist Graham Greene wrote of his journeys in the interior of Liberia in the 1920s, a place I came to know well as a United Methodist missionary. During our evacuation from the U.S. embassy during the Liberian Civil War, my family stayed in Greene's house on the adjacent, but now defunct, British Embassy grounds. While waiting for helicopters, I asked myself the kind of questions I imagined Greene would have asked, "Why am I here; why am I again on the move; where am I going now; how will the people I leave behind fare; and how do all these places and peoples find any meaning for me and my family?" In that dangerous space and time, I had few answers. After my return to the States, I read Greene's travelogue of Liberia entitled "Journeys Without Maps." He disclosed that there were some journeys made by people of faith, for which there simply are no maps. Moreover, mapping uncharted territory of any kind requires living and learning patiently, as one discovers meaning from movement on a journey. This historical atlas, like any theology that takes the world seriously, is a type of map made by one in motion. It is one person's patient attempt to tease meaning from the trajectories of our traditions, from the bewildering variety of people visited and places inhabited. It is an incomplete picture to be sure. But it assumes, as the apostle Paul did on one journey to Athens, that this God the nations seek is the one in which "we live and move and have our being"—wherever in the world we call our parish.

As Graham Greene quoted Oliver Wendell Homes in his preface, noting the similarities between a life and a map, so shall I:

The life of an individual is in many respects like a child's dissected map. If I could live a hundred years, keeping my intelligence to the last, I feel as if I could put the pieces together until they made a properly connected whole. As it is, I, like all others, find a certain number of connected fragments, and a larger number of disjointed pieces, which I might in time place in their natural connection. . . . With every decade I find some new pieces coming into place. Blanks which have been left in former years find their complement among the undisturbed fragments. If I could look back on the whole, as we look at the child's map when it is put together, I feel that I should have my whole life intelligently laid out before me.

So it remains that each life, and each religious movement, must be read humbly like a child's map.

If this "child's map" helps us *wonder* more at the historic journeys of the People Called Methodist and their descendants, and *wander* further through our tradition, then the atlas will have fulfilled its task.

W. Harrison Daniel, Ph.D.
Candler School of Theology
Emory University
Atlanta, Georgia

Roots of a Family Tree

A Genealogy of the Wesleyan Revival

John and Charles Wesley, contrary to stereotypes, descended from noble parliamentarians, minor landed gentry, and—above all—a long line of preachers. A direct ancestor, Sir William de Welles-ley, was elected to Parliament in 1339, to represent an area of Somerset in which he lived. He took his surname from the nearby village, Welswey (near modern-day Wells). His oldest son, Walrond, inherited the family's Wellesley Manor, while the second son, Richard, as so often happened in the period, was forced to emigrate to Ireland. There he made both name and fortune, leading the Irish line of Wellesleys, which later included Arthur Wellesley, Duke of Wellington and vanquisher of Napoleon at Waterloo.

After a number of generations with unclear sources (see opposite page), both the English (Westley) and Irish (Wellesley) lines of the family flowed together again. Sir Herbert Westley of Westleigh, Devon, married his cousin Elizabeth Wellesley, daughter of Sir Robert de Wellesley of Dangan Castle, Ireland. Their son Bartholomew was born in 1596. He entered Oxford and studied medicine, the first of the Wes-leys listed as attending Oxford. He married Ann Colley, daughter of Sir Henry Colley of Castle Car-bery, Kildare County, Ireland in 1620. Their son John Westley (note the "t") was born in 1636 and was immediately dedicated to the ministry. After practicing medicine for some years, Bartholomew him-self entered the ministry as a Puritan (English Calvinist) in the Church of England, receiving appoint-ment to Charmouth parish in 1640. After Charles II's ejection of Puritans from established churches in the Restoration beginning in 1660, Bartholomew lost his Chermouth parish but continued Noncon-formist preaching. His son John Westley trained for holy orders at Oxford and, after graduating with an M.A., simply began preaching without episcopal ordination at Winterborn-Whitchurch parish in the Presbyterian manner in 1658. He married the daughter of the great Puritan preacher John White, and the family produced a son named Samuel, born in 1662 in Dorsetshire. The Rev. John Westley soon began to undergo the same persecution of Puritans that his father had experienced and was jailed for five months. He was ejected from his Church of England parish and removed to Poole in 1662, where he preached to small Puritan gatherings until his untimely death at forty-two years old in 1678.

As a member of a prominent family of Nonconformists, Samuel obtained his education from a foremost Dissenter academy in Stepney, London. Circulating freely among Puritan families, Samuel met Susanna Annesley, daughter of the renowned Puritan Rev. Dr. Samuel Annesley, rector of Lon-don's largest parish—St. Giles Cripplegate. He too was forced to leave St. Giles and preach to Puri-tans in Little St. Helens Street. Samuel and Susanna were married in 1688, the same year he entered the ministry of the Church of England with such promise: first as curate of St. Andrew's Holborn, London; later in 1691 appointed rector of South Ormesby parish in Lincolnshire; and finally, when he arrived at Epworth parish in 1697. There, Samuel ministered until his death in 1735. There, also in that famous Lincolnshire parish, he and Susanna produced and reared two more great preachers— John and Charles Wesley—thereby adding a worldwide reach to a family tree with prominent national roots.

**▲ Susanna's London Home
& Birthplace
▼ Her Father's Dissenting
Church in Little St.Helen's**

Rev. John Westley, M.A. 1636-1678

Rev. Samuel Wesley, M.A. 1662-1735

Susanna Wesley 1669-1742

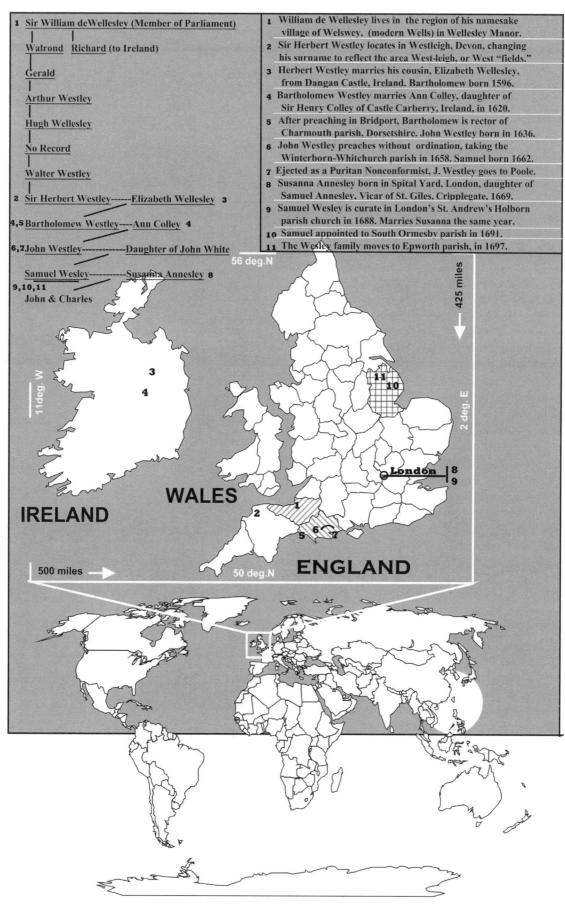

1 Sir William deWellesley (Member of Parliament)

Walrond   Richard (to Ireland)

Gerald

Arthur Westley

Hugh Wellesley

No Record

Walter Westley

2 Sir Herbert Westley------Elizabeth Wellesley 3

4,5 Bartholomew Westley----Ann Colley 4

6,7 John Westley-------------Daughter of John White

Samuel Wesley----------Susanna Annesley 8

9,10,11
John & Charles

1 William de Wellesley lives in the region of his namesake village of Welswey, (modern Wells) in Wellesley Manor.

2 Sir Herbert Westley locates in Westleigh, Devon, changing his surname to reflect the area West-leigh, or West "fields."

3 Herbert Westley marries his cousin, Elizabeth Wellesley, from Dangan Castle, Ireland. Bartholomew born 1596.

4 Bartholomew Westley marries Ann Colley, daughter of Sir Henry Colley of Castle Carberry, Ireland, in 1620.

5 After preaching in Bridport, Bartholomew is rector of Charmouth parish, Dorsetshire. John Westley born in 1636.

6 John Westley preaches without ordination, taking the Winterborn-Whitchurch parish in 1658. Samuel born 1662.

7 Ejected as a Puritan Nonconformist, J. Westley goes to Poole.

8 Susanna Annesley born in Spital Yard, London, daughter of Samuel Annesley, Vicar of St. Giles, Cripplegate, 1669.

9 Samuel Wesley is curate in London's St. Andrew's Holborn parish church in 1688. Marries Susanna the same year.

10 Samuel appointed to South Ormesby parish in 1691.

11 The Wesley family moves to Epworth parish, in 1697.

56 deg.N

425 miles

11deg. W

2 deg. E

IRELAND

WALES

3
4

London 8
9

1
2
5 6 7

ENGLAND

500 miles

50 deg.N

Epworth and Environs

Scene of the Wesley Brothers' Childhood

Samuel Wesley (who first dropped the "t") was a fair poet, better hymn writer, and even better scholar. Yet history remembers him most as the father of John and Charles Wesley. They were born to him and Susanna Annesley once he became rector of the Church of England parish in Epworth, Lincolnshire, in 1697. Though Samuel trained at Newington Green, a private school for Dissenters in preparation to become a clergyman in that movement, he later converted to the Church of England during his studies at Oxford. He and his wife, Susanna, thereafter served appointed parishes in the established church with a distinctive Puritan emphasis—though often disagreeing with each other on fine points of theological and political principle. At Epworth in Lincolnshire, the Wesleys served for thirty-eight years, living in the Old Rectory, still preserved today. There Susanna bore nineteen surviving children, including the three oldest boys: Samuel, John (born June 1703), and Charles (December 1707). All of the children were raised by Susanna, with the highest schooling available in the village—in her own home.

Lincolnshire geography has interesting features that contributed to the relationship of Samuel Wesley to his family and to the St. Andrew's parish—not to mention with the larger region centered upon the small market town of Epworth. St. Andrew's parish church was the high parish church, on the highest point for many miles on the sunken plain of the Isle of Axholme. Lincolnshire was originally an island, as the inland rivers and the Humber all connected and flowed into the North Sea. Dutch engineering developed sufficiently to drain the many rivers of Axholme and create a fertile agricultural plateau. In light of this only recent reconnection with the notion of the main British Isles, the people of this part of Lincolnshire had endured a rather fair case of isolation. This had promoted both Nonconformist religion and Whig (anti-King & Country Tory politics) sentiments in the region. These geographic and religiopolitical tendencies put the Rev. Samuel Wesley into quite a tension. Samuel and Susanna could both readily relate to the marginalization of the region, filtered through their parents' experiences as leading Puritans persecuted for their critique of the established Church of England. Yet, in light of the persecution of their parents, Samuel and Susanna both held allegiance to the established church and its theology as far as possible. Because of Samuel's religious and political affirmations, and given his geographic location, conflict within his parish was inevitable. Samuel Wesley's parishioners set fire to the Old Rectory twice—in 1702 and 1709. In the second arson, little John Wesley was rescued by a human ladder of concerned persons—after which Susanna declared that this son had a special mission as a "brand plucked from the burning." As a narrative retold both in the family and in Methodist journals, John Benjamin Wesley not only acquired a warrant for a special mission but also gained an important exposure to ecclesiastical politics that would prepare him to stomach the volatile opposition to the revival ahead.

In geographic terms, the setting has something to say about the story of the Wesleyan revival. Epworth village was the capital of Axholme: a high vantage point over a sunken, isolated, former island transformed by dams and other methods. In this context, John grew up under his father and mother's tutelage to understand that parishes, regions, churches, and therefore individuals can be transformed through attention to spiritual, educational, and communal disciplines. From the high center toward the sunken, fertile margins, the Wesleys' preaching and revival would, like Axholme in Lincolnshire, redraw the map of religious history in eighteenth-century Great Britain and the world.

1 St. Andrew's Parish Church, Epworth, served by Rev. Samuel Wesley, 1697-1735

2 The Old Rectory, birthplace of John and Charles Wesley, and where Susanna educated her children.

Feb.1709, arsonists struck the Rectory, and young John is barely rescued by a human ladder. Susanna later claimed a divine mission for her son, " I shall be more particular of the soul of this child...he is a brand plucked from the burning."

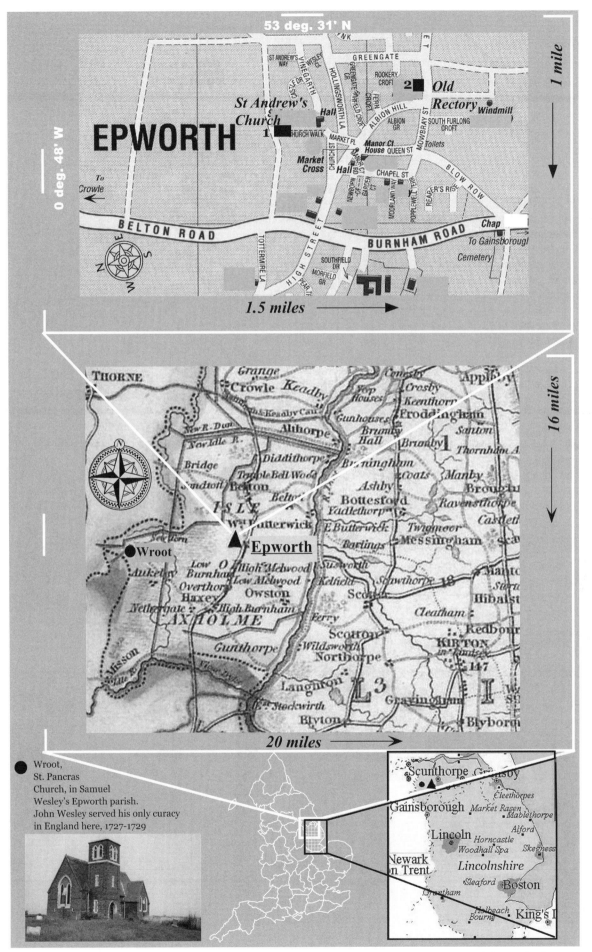

53 deg. 31' N

1 mile

0 deg. 48' W

GREENGATE

ST ANDREW'S WAY

2 **Old Rectory**

ROOKERY CROFT

Windmill

St Andrew's Church

1

CHURCH WALK

ALBION HILL

ALBION GR

SOUTH FURLONG CROFT

EPWORTH

MARKET PL

Manor Ct House

QUEEN ST

Toilets

Market Cross

Hall

CHAPEL ST

BLOW ROW

To Crowle

N W E S

BELTON ROAD

BURNHAM ROAD

Chap

To Gainsborough

Cemetery

1.5 miles →

16 miles

THORNE

Grange

Crowle

Keadby

Crosby

Keenthorpe

Froddingham

Althorpe

Brumby Hall

Brumby

Thornholm A

Bridge

Diddithorpe

Bromingham

Coats

Manby

Brought

Ashby

Bottesford

Ravensthorpe

Castleti

I S L E

Fadlethorp

W. Butterwick

▲ **Epworth**

E. Butterwick

Twigmoor

Messingham

● **Wroot**

Low O High Melwood

Susworth

Burnham

Low Melwood

Kelfield

Scawthorpe

Mant

Overthorp

Owston

Haxey

Netterfate

High Burnham

A X H O L M E

Ferry

Scotter

Cleatham

Redbour

Gunthorpe

Wildsworth

Northorpe

Scotton

KIRTON

147

Langton

L 3

Stockwith

Graringham

Blyton

Blyborо

20 miles →

● Wroot,
St. Pancras
Church, in Samuel
Wesley's Epworth parish.
John Wesley served his only curacy
in England here, 1727-1729

Scunthorpe Grimsby

● ▲

Cleethorpes

Gainsborough Market Rasen Mablethorpe

Lincoln Horncastle Alford

Woodhall Spa Skegness

Newark on Trent Lincolnshire

Sleaford Boston

Grantham

Holbeach Bourne King's I

The Three Rises of Methodism: The First Rise

Wesley Teaches Classics and Leads the Holy Club at Lincoln College, Oxford, November 1729–October 1735

In *Ecclesiastical History*, his 1781 retrospective history of Methodism, John Wesley located three key stages in the formation of the Methodist movement. He drew attention to the first, second, and third rises of Methodism as key environments that formed the Wesleyan revival. The message arose as John Wesley moved over space through time, reflecting upon his search for knowledge and vital piety in three formational settings: Oxford, Georgia, and Pietist London. These settings constituted a trajectory from the safe learning institutions of home and the high ideology of Oxford; toward the marginalized colonists and Native Americans of Georgia; and then back to the German Pietistic renewal fringe movements rooting in London. Out of these three movements Wesley and his later colleagues responded by action across many perceived boundaries of the time: not by going higher in the institutional ladders open to him, but rather by going deeper into the demographic margins of British society and connections with the wider world.

Wesley located the first rise of Methodism in his days from November 1729 to October 1735 as a fellow of Lincoln College, Oxford. Here he combined exacting scholarly teaching with leading a group of undergraduates (formed by brother Charles) to read, to learn, and to serve the poor and imprisoned in Oxford Castle and the Bocardo Prison. While renewal groups within Oxford associated with the Puritan wing of the Church of England were common, it was exceptionally rare for an ordained fellow of Oxford to lead students to take their search for assurance beyond the confines of the University. From the spire of St. Mary's to the tower of Oxford Castle, John Wesley and his Oxford Club moved easily and spread their message of God's love for all in spiritual and physical disciplined service. The Holy Club soon attracted critical notice in the Oxford press when one of its members, William Morgan, died of tuberculosis in the fall of 1732. The erroneous charge that the Holy Club was a rigorous ascetic group that mortified the flesh to achieve salvation was the first pejorative use of the word *Methodists* applied to Wesley's group. The charges were met by John Wesley through a leaked "Morgan" letter: the methods employed by the group were not to achieve salvation, but were corporate, public expressions that proved and promoted inward impressions of assured salvation.

Wesley planned to remain in Oxford and pursue a comfortable academic career path. Once he became a resident tutor in November 1729, he insisted on teaching every student every day of the year. The young don taught Greek, philosophy, and other classics, and his engagement with students made Wesley a popular lecturer. Nonetheless, Wesley remained frustrated in his attempts to find spiritual assurance through the rituals of the Holy Club. On New Year's Day 1733, Wesley preached on "The Circumcision of the Heart" at the University Church of St. Mary's. In the sermon, Wesley propounded a spiritual religion of dedication and faithful service but did not yet connect justifying faith with imparted holiness, as he would in his mature theology.

✚ **St.Mary's University Church**

◯ **Oxford Castle Prison Tower**

△ **Bocardo Prison over North Gate, St.Giles**

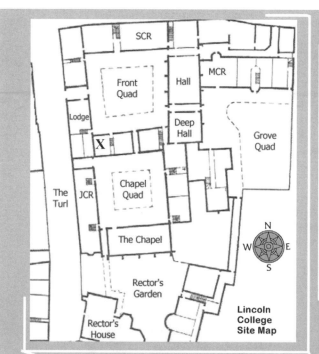

Lincoln College Site Map

SCR

Front Quad

Hall

MCR

Lodge

X

Deep Hall

Grove Quad

The Turl

JCR

Chapel Quad

The Chapel

Rector's Garden

Rector's House

X Wesley's Rooms at Lincoln College, overlooking the Front Quad, where the Oxford Holy Club met 1729–1735

51 deg. 45' N

1 deg. 15' W

St. Mary's University Church

Lincoln College

High Street

Lincoln College Oxford Univeristy

New Road

St. Aldate's

Lane

Merton Street

High Street

Christ Church Cathedral

Oxford, England

Dundee

Glasgow • • Edinburgh

Newcastle Upon Tyne

Ulster

Liverpool

Birmingham • • Leicester

Oxford

Cambridge

Bristol •

London

St. Mary's Church is the University Church for all of Oxford. As an Oxford don (professor), Wesley was required to preach here once every three years, in which he complied from 1733 to 1744. In his last sermon, "On Scriptural Christianity," he accused Oxford of being neither a Christian city nor institution. He was never invited to preach at St. Mary's again.

Wesley's Rooms from the Front Quad looking south

X

The Second Rise of Methodism

The Wesley Brothers Serve as Missionaries in Oglethorpe's Georgia, 1736–1737

"A Parish of above 200 miles laughs at the labor of one man."

—John Wesley

Why would a popular Oxford don with academic tenure leave the dreaming spires of the university to serve as a missionary in the doubtful British colony of Georgia? Bedtime stories from mother Susanna about missionaries to India were clearly an early stimulus. Yet as a member of the relatively elite clergy in the Church of England, John Wesley also received overtures from the highest leaders of the Society for the Propagation of the Gospel in Foreign Parts. The SPG formed the Church of England's "foreign office," supporting Great Britain's colonial initiatives by supplying chaplains. Georgia, as the last of the original colonies, was established for Britain's "worthy poor" as an alternative to debtor's prison. Yet perhaps more important, it existed as a buffer to protect other British colonies against Spanish invasion from the south. As a British crown colony, only Church of England priests could be placed in charge of its spiritual well-being.

On December 2, 1735, John and Charles Wesley, along with Charles Delamotte and Benjamin Ingham, set sail from Gravesend, England, for the colony of Georgia as missionary clergy of the SPG. After a three-month journey that included three violent storms, the last occurring only one week before sighting the Georgia shore (1), Wesley's veneer as the strong, faithful pastor of the company crumbled under cumulative and combined effects: First, from his physical difficulties with fighting the elements; and second, from his vulnerable lack of spiritual assurance in relation to his newfound friends, the Moravian Brethren. Wesley wished to preach the gospel to the Yamacraw Indians largely to confirm his own assurance and understanding of that gospel. After landing on February 6, 1736 (2), and leading General Oglethorpe and company in prayers on the marshy Peeper (now Cockspur) Island (across from today's luxury resort of Tybee Island), Wesley's ship *The Simmons* proceeded up the Savannah River to the oldest city in colonial Georgia (3). At the time, there was no church building for the Anglicans in the colony. A small parsonage and garden were provided for Wesley, who preached initially at the Customs House and then later at President and Whitaker streets, before Christ Church Episcopal was erected on the lot at Johnson Square. Brother Charles soon located at the southern end of the two-hundred-mile parish, as General Oglethorpe's secretary for Indian affairs resident in Fort Frederica and its settlement on Great St. Simon's Island (4). Charles was the priest for the settlement but was theologically and politically unsure in relation to the parishioners and Governor Oglethorpe. Wesley journeyed five times to preach in Frederica and quickly learned languages to lead services for his diverse spiritual charges, including Moravians in Bethesda; Salzburg Protestants at Ebenezer; Scottish settlers at Darien and further north at Ft. Argyle; as well as the Jews of Savannah and the Yamacraw Indians of the Creek Nation. Oglethorpe rejected John Wesley's well-organized plan to evangelize the Creeks of the interior, arguing that his efforts were needed to keep the social and spiritual order of the colony's main towns. This galled Wesley deeply, who went to Georgia primarily to minister to Native Americans. Both Charles and John felt that Oglethorpe had been disingenuous about the political reasons for their ministry in the colony. Charles saw that administering Indian affairs from the colonial perspective was more about managing the natives into submission for the interests of the crown than teaching the gospel in the noncoercive way the Indians requested. Frustrated, Charles left in July 1736. Wesley's dogged determination to keep the entire two-hundred-mile parish under strong ecclesial discipline aroused the ire of many of the colony's inhabitants. He was often absent from Savannah. His soap-opera missteps in youthful love for Sophia Hopkey, niece of the Magistrate of the Court, culminated in Wesley's denial of the sacraments to his former love interest and her new husband. Because doing so carried legal as well as ecclesiastical consequences for Sophy, her uncle retaliated by issuing a warrant for Wesley's arrest. Under the cover of night, he slipped over to Charleston and sailed home for England in December 1737. None of his real accomplishments among the colonists and slaves were apparent to Wesley as he sailed home. As he left, he wrote, "I came to America to convert the heathens, but oh who will convert me. . . . I left America, having preached not as I ought, but as I was able."

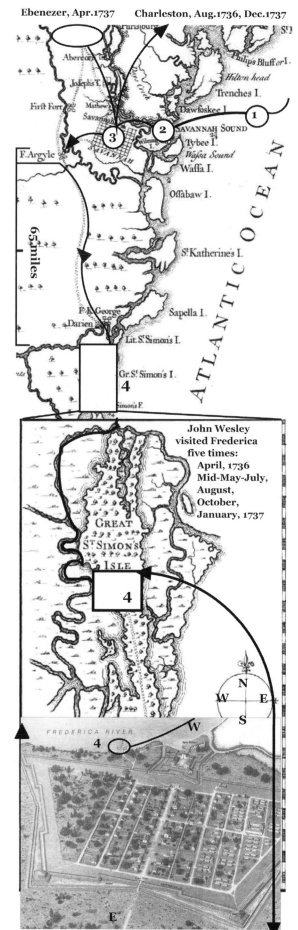

John Wesley visited Frederica five times:
April, 1736
Mid-May-July,
August,
October,
January, 1737

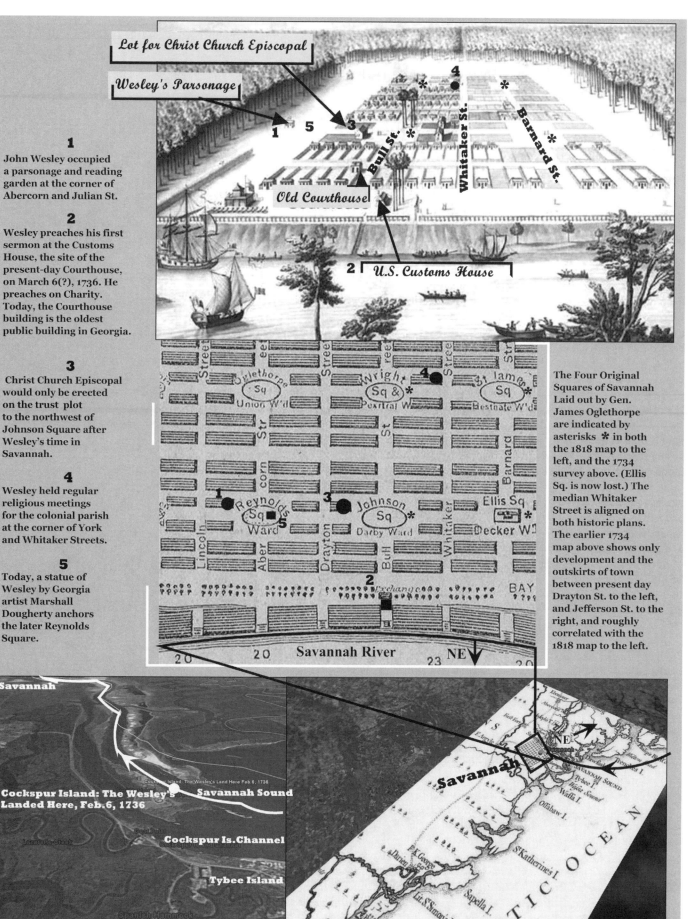

Lot for Christ Church Episcopal

Wesley's Parsonage

1

5 3

4

Bull St.

Whitaker St.

Barnard St.

Old Courthouse

2 U.S. Customs House

1

John Wesley occupied a parsonage and reading garden at the corner of Abercorn and Julian St.

2

Wesley preaches his first sermon at the Customs House, the site of the present-day Courthouse, on March 6(?), 1736. He preaches on Charity. Today, the Courthouse building is the oldest public building in Georgia.

3

Christ Church Episcopal would only be erected on the trust plot to the northwest of Johnson Square after Wesley's time in Savannah.

4

Wesley held regular religious meetings for the colonial parish at the corner of York and Whitaker Streets.

5

Today, a statue of Wesley by Georgia artist Marshall Dougherty anchors the later Reynolds Square.

The Four Original Squares of Savannah Laid out by Gen. James Oglethorpe are indicated by asterisks ✱ in both the 1818 map to the left, and the 1734 survey above. (Ellis Sq. is now lost.) The median Whitaker Street is aligned on both historic plans. The earlier 1734 map above shows only development and the outskirts of town between present day Drayton St. to the left, and Jefferson St. to the right, and roughly correlated with the 1818 map to the left.

Oglethorpe Sq

Wright Sq &

St. James Sq

Union W'd

Central W

Bestnate W'da

Reynolds Sq

Johnson Sq

Ellis Sq

Ward

Darby Ward

Decker W

Exchange

BAY

20   20   Savannah River   23 NE   20

Savannah

Cockspur Island: The Wesley's Landed Here, Feb. 6, 1736

Savannah Sound

Cockspur Is. Channel

Tybee Island

Savannah

NE

SAVANNAH SOUND

ATLANTIC OCEAN

The Third Rise of Methodism

Wesley's London and Religious Societies

"Christians [in Britain] . . . were more savage . . . than the wildest Indians I have yet met."
—John Wesley

Charles Wesley returned to Britain on December 3, 1736, and John arrived on February 1, 1738. Arriving in Deal at four in the morning, John set out for London later that day. He caught his first glimpse of English life after his absence in America and of the need for a great revival of true religion in his native land. "I here read prayers, and explained the Second Lesson, to a few of those who were called Christians but were indeed, more savage in their behaviour than the wildest Indians I have yet met with" (*Journals and Diaries*, 18:221).

John and Charles returned to a London undergoing particular geographic, spiritual, and demographic changes. While only London Bridge spanned the Thames River until the eighteenth century, once more bridges were built, the city spread rapidly in all directions, as the low, rolling hills surrounding the river in all directions posed no barrier to growth. The rapid expansion of the city in conjunction with the steady industrialization of Britain in the early eighteenth century, pushed many rural poor into the city, promoting squalid conditions, drunkenness, debt, poverty, and crime. Such conditions were well represented in William Hogarth's prints. Additionally, the Church of England was slow to deal with the spiritual and physical degradation of urbanization as large numbers of people immigrated to the cities. Church of England ministry practices and polity were deeply entrenched in the slow, rural, stable rhythms of the parish systems. The church's parishes in both the rural countryside and in London could not keep up with the rapid movement of parishioners toward and through the city.

Immediately following the last Great Plague, 1665–1666, and the Great Fire of London, 1666, London had experienced a considerable religious awakening through the use of small religious societies loosely related to official parishes. By 1699, about forty societies existed across London, mainly consisting of young persons seeking assurance of salvation through faith. Also, twenty different associations were formed to suppress the town's debilitating spiritual and physical conditions. By the time the Wesleys returned to London, few of these societies remained vital, mainly those stimulated by the new Moravian influx into the city. John and Charles were quickly able to tap into this network of societies that met first at James Hutton's shop (A), then Fetter Lane (B), and Aldersgate Street (C) (see map, p. 17).

The Moravians were an outgrowth of the United Brethren (*Unitas Fratum*), a group that first arose under John Hus in the 1400s as a resistance effort to perceived Catholic oppression in Moravia and Bohemia (modern Czech Republic). In 1467, the Moravians broke away from Rome. In 1722, Moravians sought refuge in a village named Herrnhut (the Lord's Watch) on the estate of Count Nicholas Zinzendorf of Saxony. Further persecution in Saxony (from Catholicism and state Lutheranism) forced Zinzendorf into exile, and many Moravians were forced to relocate in Britain and in Georgia in the 1730s.

London was a diverse religious ecology when the Wesleys returned to seek a place among often competing societies—such as the Moravians and those groups influenced by the Church of England. After Charles and John's reunion on February 3, 1738, in London, both men met the Moravian preacher Peter Boehler on February 7. The Wesleys conversed deeply with him in London and Oxford on many occasions throughout the spring about their lack of assured salvation by faith. Out of these discussions Wesley queried Boehler, on March 5 in Oxford, "But what can I preach?" to which Boehler replied, "Preach faith till you have it, and then because you have it, you will preach faith" (*Journals and Diaries*, 18:228). Tensions developed after meetings with the Bishop of London and the Archbishop of Canterbury, when the Wesleys were advised against teaching assurance and adult rebaptism, two beliefs at the heart of the Moravian message. Nevertheless, Charles experienced assurance of faith on May 21, 1738, in Little Britain after reading Luther's Preface to Galatians; John found his heart "strangely warmed" by visiting a society in Nettleton Court, Aldersgate Street, three days later on May 24. Here Wesley wrote, after the reading of Luther's Preface to Romans: "I felt I did trust in Christ, Christ alone for salvation, and an assurance was given me that he had taken away my sins, even mine, and saved me from the law of sin and death" (*Journals and Diaries*, 18:249-50). The heart strangely warmed quickly grew cold, and Wesley embarked on a spiritual pilgrimage to meet Count Zinzendorf in Germany. Regardless of his heart's temperature, this assured faith put John Wesley in motion, keeping him running for the next fifty years.

Hogarth's Print "Gin Lane"

Zinzendorf's Herrnhut

Peter Boehler

Nettleton Ct. Aldersgate Street

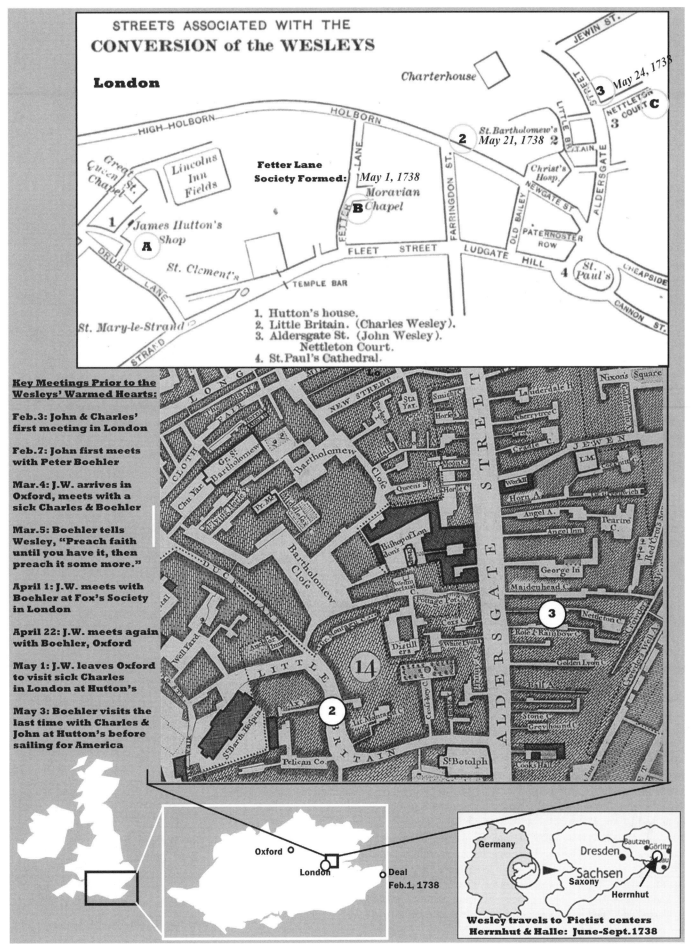

STREETS ASSOCIATED WITH THE
CONVERSION of the WESLEYS

London

Charterhouse

St. Bartholomew's
May 21, 1738

May 24, 1738

Fetter Lane Society Formed: *May 1, 1738*
Moravian Chapel

Christ's Hosp.

James Hutton's Shop

St. Clement's

TEMPLE BAR

1. Hutton's house.
2. Little Britain. (Charles Wesley).
3. Aldersgate St. (John Wesley).
   Nettleton Court.
4. St. Paul's Cathedral.

Key Meetings Prior to the Wesleys' Warmed Hearts:

Feb. 3: John & Charles' first meeting in London

Feb. 7: John first meets with Peter Boehler

Mar. 4: J.W. arrives in Oxford, meets with a sick Charles & Boehler

Mar. 5: Boehler tells Wesley, "Preach faith until you have it, then preach it some more."

April 1: J.W. meets with Boehler at Fox's Society in London

April 22: J.W. meets again with Boehler, Oxford

May 1: J.W. leaves Oxford to visit sick Charles in London at Hutton's

May 3: Boehler visits the last time with Charles & John at Hutton's before sailing for America

Oxford

London

Deal Feb. 1, 1738

Germany

Dresden

Bautzen

Görlitz

Sachsen

Saxony

Herrnhut

Wesley travels to Pietist centers Herrnhut & Halle: June-Sept. 1738

The Reluctant Revivalist

Wesley Joins Whitefield in Bristol and Preaches Faith in the Fields, but Quickly Builds Preaching Houses

George Whitefield, 1714-1770

"I began expounding our Lord's Sermon on the Mount (one pretty remarkable precedent of field preaching)."
—John Wesley

John Wesley arrived back in London from the Continent on Saturday evening, September 16, 1738, and preached the following morning at Holy Trinity in the Minories. From September 1738 through March 1739, John and Charles preached regularly in the little societies of Fetter Lane, Aldersgate, and Gutter Lane, as well as Newgate Prison. Additionally John preached at St. Anne's and St. John's Churches, and Charles was briefly but unsuccessfully curate in Islington. Both soon experienced resistance from parishioners and clergy. John's message of justification by faith was coldly met in February at St. Giles Cripplegate and later in March at Wheeler's Chapel in Spitalfields. The Wesleys were faced with a tough decision after meeting with the Bishop of London and the Archbishop of Canterbury: follow the Moravians and preach their message of assured faith and risk charges of "enthusiasm," or capitulate to a moderate establisment theology based on the *via media* of the Thirty-Nine Articles. While churches and bishops closed down preaching opportunities for the Wesleys, George Whitefield had also been turned out of many Anglican churches and consequently had begun to preach in the fields in Bristol. Despite Whitefield's success in Bristol, Bath, and the infamous collieries of Kingswood, he desired to return to America. He therefore invited John to Bristol to carry on his field preaching. Arriving on Saturday, March 31, Wesley met with Whitefield. The following Sunday morning April 1, John watched Whitefield preach outdoors during the day, with some misgivings about this strange breach of ecclesial protocol. Wesley wrote in his diary, "I could scarcely reconcile myself at first to this strange way of preaching in the fields . . . having been all my life (till very lately) so tenacious of every point relating to decency in order, that I should have thought the saving of souls almost a sin, if it had not been done in a church" (*Journals and Diaries,* 19:46). That evening in a little society in Nicholas Street (1) (see map, p. 21), Wesley preached on the Sermon on the Mount, what he termed "one pretty remarkable precedent of field preaching, though I suppose there were churches at that time also" (*Journals and Diaries*, 19:46). The following day Wesley entered the field, taking the text of Luke 4:18-19—the inauguration of Christ's ministry. He preached on "a little eminence" outside the city to around three thousand persons. Wesley quickly expanded his area of operations by preaching in the fields of Bath, Kingswood, and Bristol, and in both the Nicholas and Baldwin Street (2) societies. The following preaching plan, found in Wesley's diary, demonstrates his regular itineration to saturate the population over the period from April to June 1739: Every morning: Newgate Prison. Monday afternoon: Bristol (Nicholas and Baldwin Street societies). Tuesday: Bath and Two Mile Hill (on the road between Bristol and Kingswood). Wednesday: Baptist Mills (just east of Bristol). Every other Thursday: Pensford. Every other Friday: Kingswood. Saturday afternoon and Sunday morning: Bowling Green (near Bristol city center). Sunday 11 AM: Hanham Mount (southwest of Kingswood). 2 PM: Clifton (west end of Bristol). 5 PM: Rose Green (just east of Bristol). This rapid and regular preaching in a city that was at the time the second largest in Britain had produced critical mass by May 12. Here, Wesley's inclinations toward regular preaching indoors showed, as he quickly underwrote the cost of building the first chapel in Methodism: the New Rooms, located in a courtyard between the Horsefair and Broadmead (3). Wesley returned to London in mid-June. He made a total of four journeys from London to Bristol in 1739. He visited Oxford four times and had a short stay in Wales. Thus, in his inaugural year of ministry, the first three months of 1739 were mainly spent in London; then Wesley was in Bristol for a total of five months. He finished out the year with two more months devoted late that year to London. But already before the end of the summer, Methodism had spread between London and Bristol, reaching even into Wales. Bristol proved to be a strategic geographic gateway to the western parts of Britain. From Bristol, the Wesleys could easily set out into Somerset, Devon, and Cornwall. Bristol was likewise often the starting point for journeys into Wales and across to Ireland. It formed one of the three focal points of John Wesley's many journeys between London (A), Newcastle, and the West Country. Another important center of gravity for the movement emerged in November 1739, when Wesley purchased an old foundry along City Road in London, as he was breaking with the leadership of the Moravian societies. The Wesleyan revival now had roots in the two largest population centers and was poised to reach into every corner of the British Isles. The Methodists had spread to every part of Britain except Shetland by Wesley's death in 1791.

Wesley Preaches in Open, Bristol, 1739

3 New Rooms, Bristol, May 1739

A The Foundery, London, Nov.1739

B Wesley Chapel, City Rd, London, 1778

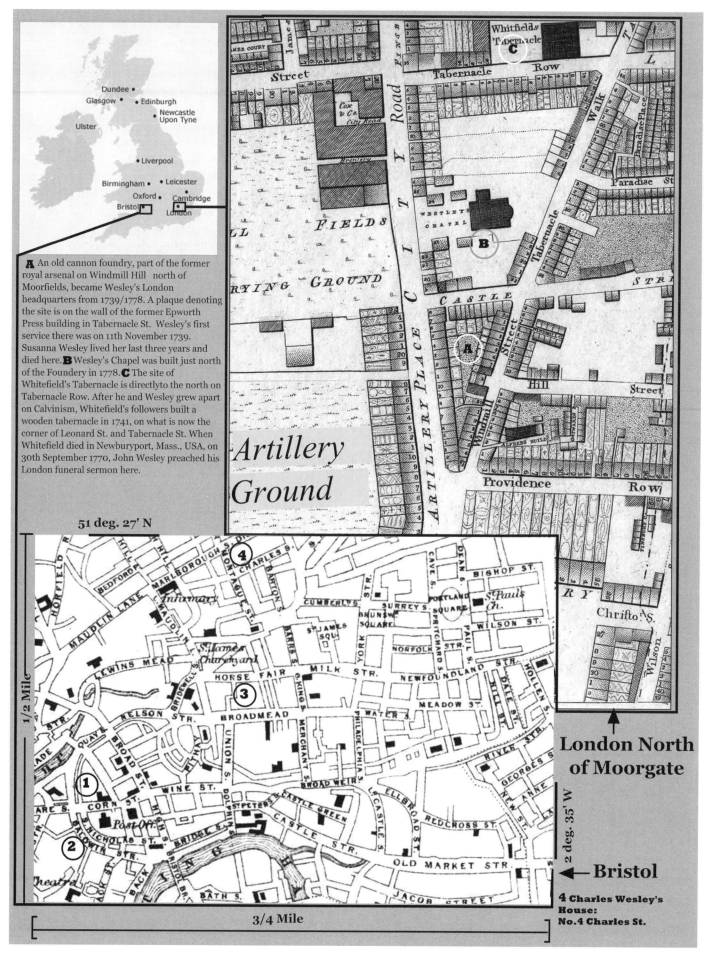

A An old cannon foundry, part of the former royal arsenal on Windmill Hill north of Moorfields, became Wesley's London headquarters from 1739/1778. A plaque denoting the site is on the wall of the former Epworth Press building in Tabernacle St. Wesley's first service there was on 11th November 1739. Susanna Wesley lived her last three years and died here. **B** Wesley's Chapel was built just north of the Foundery in 1778. **C** The site of Whitefield's Tabernacle is directly to the north on Tabernacle Row. After he and Wesley grew apart on Calvinism, Whitefield's followers built a wooden tabernacle in 1741, on what is now the corner of Leonard St. and Tabernacle St. When Whitefield died in Newburyport, Mass., USA, on 30th September 1770, John Wesley preached his London funeral sermon here.

51 deg. 27' N

Artillery Ground

London North of Moorgate

1/2 Mile

3/4 Mile

2 deg. 35' W

← **Bristol**

4 Charles Wesley's House: No.4 Charles St.

Expansion and Connexion: The Wesleyan Revival Weaves a Web of Community Up to the First Annual Conference--1738–1744

Up until 1742 Wesley's work was chiefly confined to London and Bristol, along with the adjacent places between them. On his way to Newcastle that year Wesley visited Birstal, where John Nelson, the stonemason, had already been working. On his return Wesley preached from his father's tomb at Epworth. In the summer of 1743 Charles Wesley visited Wednesbury, Leeds and Newcastle. Next year in 1744, he took Cornwall by storm. Meanwhile, the work in London was prospering.

The revival was clearly sustained by teamwork among many lay preachers.

Scotland

Ireland

WALES

56 deg.N

50 deg.N

11deg. W

2 deg. E

425 miles

Lines of Advance:
Date & First Preacher
J.W.=John Wesley
C.W.=Charles Wesley
B.I.= Benjamin Ingham
H.H.= Howell Harris
D.T.= David Taylor
J.B.= John Bennett
J.N.=John Nelson
T.M.= Thomas Maxwell
J.C.=John Cennick

Newcastle
JW:May 1742
Orphan House
Headquarters
Dec.1742
CW 1743

Knaresborough 1742
JW

Leeds 1743
CW/JW

Bradford,1739
JW/CW

Halifax,
Dewsbury Moor
Mirfield
JW:1742

Manchester, 1743, JW

Sheffield, 1742
JW

Doncaster 1743
JW

Wycombe
CW1739

N. Wales,1738, H.H.

Egginton, Derby 1743
JW

Beeston 1742
JW

Wednesbury 1743
CW/JW

Walsall & Birmingham
1743 CW

S. Wales,1739, JW

Stratford-Avon, JW:1742

Newport, Wales, JW:1742

Bristol
George Whitfield, Bristol, 1738
John Wesley, Bristol, Bath
Kingswood:1739, CW from 1739
JC:1740 Kingswood School

London:
JW/CW:1738
TM: Foundery,1740

Reading, J.W.,1739

Donnington, JW: 1742

St.Ives, 1738
D.T.
Penzance, 1739

ENGLAND

500 miles ➡

The First Conference of the Wesleyan Revival was held at the Foundry, London, June 1744. Six preachers were present, five of whom were ordained clergy of the Church of England: John and Charles Wesley, John Hodges, Rector of Wenvo, Henry Piers, Vicar of Bexley, Samuel Taylor, Vicar of Quinton, and lay preacher John Meriton.

After five years of itineration, the statistics: 45 preachers, 5 ordained C. of E. Largest society: London, c. 2,000 members. Bristol, Newcastle, and St.Ives ranked 2-4. Correlations: Cities undergoing rapid social change where John and Charles Wesley both preached in a sustained pattern showed the strongest growth. Except for marginalized Wales and the southwest counties, the London-Bristol-Newcastle triangle formed the Methodist center of gravity. From this triangle circuits and enduring patterns of Methodist itineration emerged.

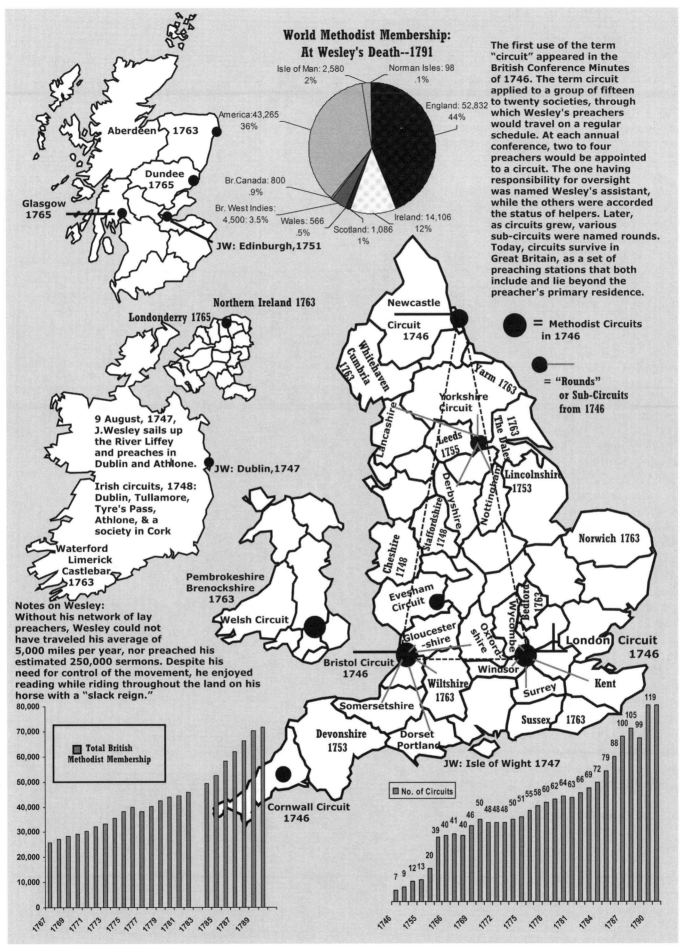

World Methodist Membership: At Wesley's Death--1791

Isle of Man: 2,580 2%
Norman Isles: 98 .1%
America: 43,265 36%
England: 52,832 44%
Br. Canada: 800 .9%
Br. West Indies: 4,500: 3.5%
Wales: 566 .5%
Scotland: 1,086 1%
Ireland: 14,106 12%

The first use of the term "circuit" appeared in the British Conference Minutes of 1746. The term circuit applied to a group of fifteen to twenty societies, through which Wesley's preachers would travel on a regular schedule. At each annual conference, two to four preachers would be appointed to a circuit. The one having responsibility for oversight was named Wesley's assistant, while the others were accorded the status of helpers. Later, as circuits grew, various sub-circuits were named rounds. Today, circuits survive in Great Britain, as a set of preaching stations that both include and lie beyond the preacher's primary residence.

Aberdeen 1763
Dundee 1765
Glasgow 1765
JW: Edinburgh, 1751

Northern Ireland 1763
Londonderry 1765

9 August, 1747, J.Wesley sails up the River Liffey and preaches in Dublin and Athlone.
JW: Dublin, 1747

Irish circuits, 1748: Dublin, Tullamore, Tyre's Pass, Athlone, & a society in Cork

Waterford Limerick Castlebar 1763

Pembrokeshire Brenockshire 1763
Welsh Circuit

Notes on Wesley:
Without his network of lay preachers, Wesley could not have traveled his average of 5,000 miles per year, nor preached his estimated 250,000 sermons. Despite his need for control of the movement, he enjoyed reading while riding throughout the land on his horse with a "slack reign."

Newcastle Circuit 1746
Whitehaven Cumbria 1762
Yarm 1763
Yorkshire Circuit
1763 The Dales
Lancashire
Leeds 1755
Lincolnshire 1753
Derbyshire
Nottingham
Staffordshire 1748
Cheshire 1748
Norwich 1763
Evesham Circuit
Bedford 1763
Wycombe
Gloucester-shire
Oxford-shire
London Circuit 1746
Bristol Circuit 1746
Windsor
Kent
Wiltshire 1763
Surrey
Somersetshire
Sussex 1763
Devonshire 1753
Dorset Portland
JW: Isle of Wight 1747
Cornwall Circuit 1746

= Methodist Circuits in 1746
= "Rounds" or Sub-Circuits from 1746

Total British Methodist Membership

80,000
70,000
60,000
50,000
40,000
30,000
20,000
10,000
0

1767 1769 1771 1773 1775 1777 1779 1781 1783 1785 1787 1789

No. of Circuits

7 9 12 13 20 39 40 41 40 46 50 48 48 48 50 51 55 58 60 62 64 63 66 69 72 79 88 100 105 99 119

1746 1755 1766 1769 1772 1775 1778 1781 1784 1787 1790

The Gift of Gab

Irish Preachers and the Lay Origins of American Methodism

About twenty miles southwest of Limerick, Ireland, lies a district known as the Palatine. Lutheran Protestant refugees settled there in the early 1700s after French Catholic forces harassed and displaced them from their home region of the Palatinate on the West Bank of the Rhine.

England and then Ireland provided asylum to the Palatines, and many of them experienced spiritual renewal when they encountered Methodism. In 1752, Wesley appointed local preachers to the Palatines, with great success. As a result, a Methodist society emerged at Castle Matrix near Rathkeale. A number of the Palatines had become Methodists already by 1760; among them was Philip Embury, who often preached in the Castle Matrix society. A group of Palatines touched by Methodism found the prospects for career and spiritual advancement more attractive in the New World. So people like Philip and Margaret Embury, brothers John, David, Peter, and their cousin Barbara Heck, along with her husband Paul, sailed from Limerick down the river Shannon, and on to New York harbor, arriving in August 1760. Other important Irish Palatines converted by Wesley were Robert and Leonard Strawbridge from Drumsna. After serving as a Methodist preacher in Terryhoogan, Ireland, Robert emigrated along with his wife Elizabeth to Sam's Creek, Maryland, America, in the early 1760s. The story of New York and Maryland Methodist lay origins owed nothing to Wesley's direction.

Once the County Limerick settlers arrived in New York, the business of making a living took precedence over creating a Methodist society. The Emburys lived first in rented quarters on 10 Augustus Street, but soon settled in Barracks Street (today's Chambers Street, ten doors away from the military barracks in the park where Broadway and Chambers Street intersect (2) (see map, p. 22). Challenged by Barbara Heck to preach to the company, "lest they all go to Hell," Philip Embury, in October 1766, once more took up his Methodist preaching in his home. In 1767, the society outgrew the home, and they acquired premises in a Rigging Loft on Horse and Cart Street (now 120 Williams Street) (3). Not long afterward, on March 30, 1768, two lots on nearby John Street were purchased from the widow of the rector of Trinity Episcopal Church (1). The first building erected on this site named Golden Hill was called Wesley Chapel and was dedicated on October 30, 1768. Here, at 44 John Street, the first Methodist chapel in America was built (4). The original church was remodeled in 1817 and the present church dates to 1841. As the Methodist church closest to the World Trade Center, John Street United Methodist Church provided safe haven and counseling for the traumatized. John Street is truly ground zero for Methodist history and, since 9/11, for our country.

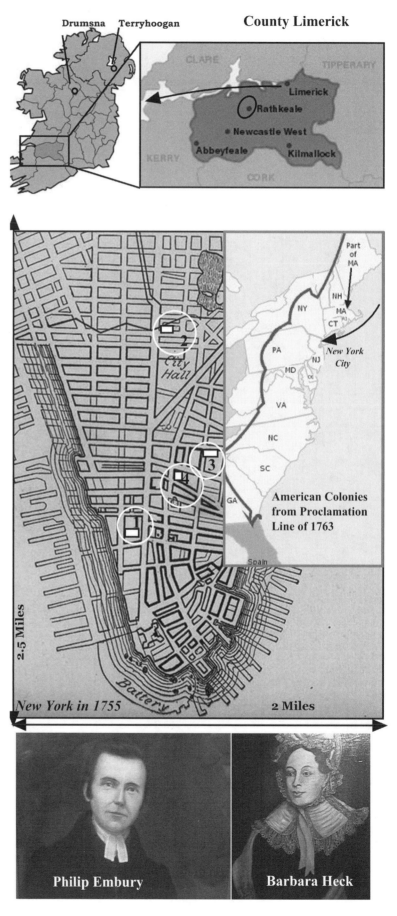

Robert Strawbridge

Sometime from 1760, Robert Strawbridge and his wife Elizabeth settled in Frederick (now Carroll) County, Maryland. They settled about 1.5 miles south[1] of present day New Windsor, MD, in between the watershed of Sam's Creek and Little Pipe Creek. He preached first in his cabin home, then formed the first circuit in 1762. Strawbridge organized the first American Methodist <u>societies</u> around 1763 or 1764. John Evans (1734-1827), first American convert of Elizabeth Strawbridge's, led the first class from 1768-1804. Strawbridge also built a log meeting house at Sam's Creek possibly as early as 1764, but perhaps as late as 1766.[2] This gave way in 1783 to another log house on Pipe's Creek called Poulson's Chapel.[3] A stone chapel succeeded it in 1800.[4] Straw-bridge also founded Bush Forest Chapel in 1768 near Aberdeen.[5] Strawbridge's neighbors farmed for him, while he preached widely through eastern Maryland, Virginia, and Pennsylvania.

Through his effective preaching, wide itineration, and irregular practice of Eucharist, he converted more persons than any other preacher of his period. Strawbridge not only raised the first generation of American Methodist preachers, but was the preacher that formed the oldest chapels in Maryland. By his death in 1781, most of Maryland had Methodist circuits, becoming an early center of gravity for American Methodism.

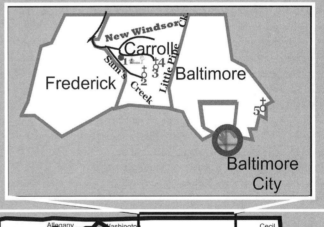

2 Log Chapel, Sam's Creek: 1764?/1766
3 Poulson's Chapel, Little Pipe's Creek:1783
4 Stone Chapel, Little Pipe's Creek: 1800

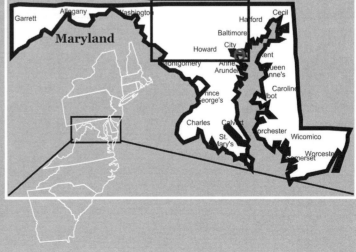

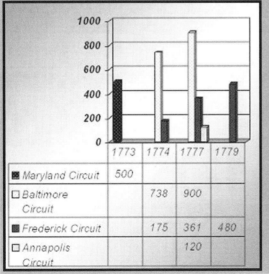

	1773	1774	1777	1779
▨ Maryland Circuit	500			
☐ Baltimore Circuit		738	900	
▦ Frederick Circuit		175	361	480
☐ Annapolis Circuit			120	

A Weaving Webb

Thomas Webb and the Foundations of a Methodist Connection

Captain Thomas Webb (c.1726–1796) was probably born in Bristol, although it is unclear. He enlisted in the British army in 1745 and in 1754 was commissioned for service in North America. He saw action under General Wolfe in the 1759 British victory over the French at Quebec, which decided Anglo dominance in British North America. Webb lost an eye and wore a patch the rest of his life. Webb settled in New York where he was appointed "barrack-master" at Albany. During a visit to England in 1765 he was converted under Moravian influence and joined the Methodists in the Bristol area.

On his return to North America, Webb became active in leading services for his troops. He caught word that a Methodist society was flourishing in New York. He visited, and presented himself to leader Philip Embury, probably while the society was meeting on Barracks Street—given his familiarity with the barracks district of New York. He soon nicely complemented Embury's preaching in the Rigging Loft on 120 Horse and Cart Street. Early reports depict his preaching as fiery, yet earnestly based on sharing the example of his transformed experience. Webb appeared in public, and indeed preached in full British officer regalia. He would dramatically open the Scriptures and then unsheathe his sword, laying it on the pulpit as a strong symbol of the power of proclamation, as well as the orders given to all officers and troops who would serve in the "King's Campaign's against the Enemy." John Adams admitted that Webb was the most moving preacher he had heard. Yet Webb was not a mere exhibitionist; he was prepared like a good barracks master to build shelters and supply his troops. He thus took a leading part in the building of the first John Street Chapel in 1768. He also negotiated the purchase of an unfinished church shell from the German Reformed Church, using his negotiation skills and military pension to purchase St. George's Chapel in Philadelphia in 1769. While a church builder and quartermaster for the Methodists of America, he took his war trauma and poured his energies into itinerating perhaps as widely as Strawbridge. He conducted preaching tours that introduced Methodism to parts of upper New York State, Long Island, New Jersey, Delaware, and Pennsylvania. Detained during the Revolutionary War for loyalist sympathies, he returned to England in 1778 and settled in Bristol where he played a key role in the founding of the Portland Methodist Chapel.

William Warren Sweet asserted in his book *Methodism and American History* that Webb was the most underappreciated agent in prerevolutionary Methodism. Both John Wesley in Britain, and the lay leaders of early New York Methodism thought him more zealous than learned. Nevertheless, Webb leveraged his experiences to not only preach a muscular Methodism woven across the colonies, but he put his money where his faithful mouth was. Webb left the earliest American Methodist societies better sheltered, financed, motivated, and connected.

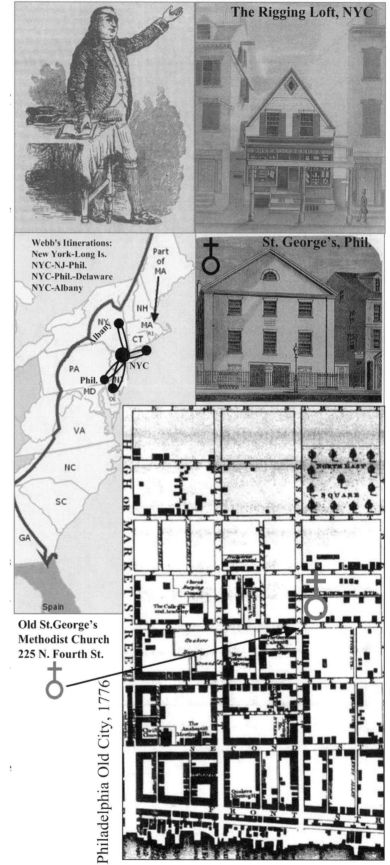

Old St. George's Methodist Church 225 N. Fourth St.

Philadelphia Old City, 1776

Wesley's Ark

British Missionaries Sent to America Two by Two to Promote Connection and Protect Control

Lay leader Thomas Taylor at John Street wrote to John Wesley in April 1768 to report the defects of Webb and Embury. In his letter, Taylor expressed an earnest desire for Wesley to send an approved and accomplished Methodist preacher to America—but would only go so far as to promise support for the preacher's sea passage. Thus, before Methodism was even a church, tensions between lay leadership and its preachers already had arisen—all the more ironic since Webb was actually the most prominent financial backer and trustee. In Methodist tradition, church politics precedes even the formation of the Methodist Church! Wesley did not immediately act, fearing sending good preachers to America would weaken the fast pace of growth in British Methodism. It was not until the following conference in Leeds, 1769, that Wesley put out a call for volunteer missionaries for America. Whereas Wesley did not confer with preachers about their circuit appointments, the American colonies—what Wesley called "Circuit Number 50"—was clearly a new frontier. Wesley set a precedent. Preachers appointed within their conference were sent; missionaries beyond conference boundaries volunteered. Such geographical distinctions remain important for polity and appointment making today in our global church.

The first volunteers were Richard Boardman and Joseph Pilmore, thirty-one and thirty years old, respectively. While Wesley's preachers in Britain were "the worst paid preachers in Britain"—the financial and faith futures of Wesley's first missionaries in the New World could not have been more uncertain. They landed six miles south of Philadelphia at Gloucester Point, New Jersey, in October 1769. Pilmore preached first and preferentially in Philadelphia, while embarking on a southern tour in 1772. Boardman oriented more naturally to New York and made an unsuccessful tour of New England in 1772. A Welshman, Robert Williams, who had a lesser authority conferred upon him after Irish itineration, had arrived under his own initiative about a month earlier in Norfolk, Virginia. Also, another uncommissioned preacher, John King, arrived in Philadelphia late in 1769. At first resisted by Pilmore, once King preached, a license was readily granted. These four preachers from late 1769 fanned out from Philadelphia, New York, and Norfolk, preaching in all the colonies before the Revolutionary War.

Wesley thereafter sent two preachers out in various years, either to replace those returning, to consolidate gains made, to push itinerants out of the comforts of the cities, or to relieve authority. His motivation seems to have been a mixture of projecting the connection further from the cities, while protecting more deeply his own control:

- 1771: Francis Asbury and Richard Wright (little known)
- 1773: Thomas Rankin and George Shadford
- 1774: John Dempster (NY) and Martin Rodda (briefly in MD)

During the eight-year period of Wesley's missionary approach to America (1769–1777), circuit number 50 grew considerably with deeper preaching penetration outside the largest cities. By the end of 1777, all British preachers except Asbury and King had either died or returned home, due to their perceived or real sympathies with Britain.

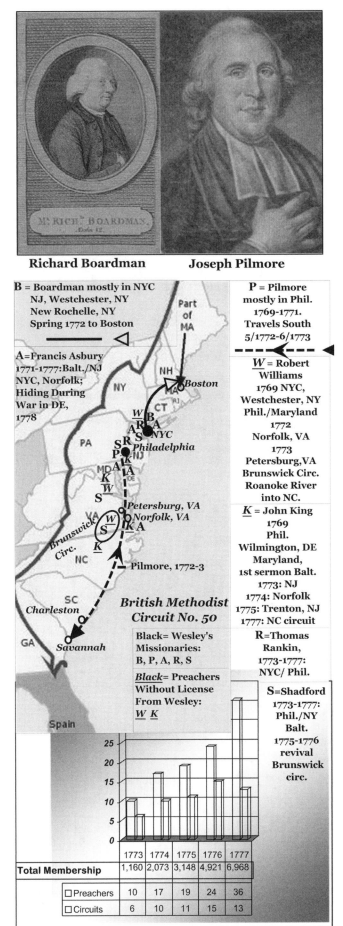

Richard Boardman **Joseph Pilmore**

B = Boardman mostly in NYC NJ, Westchester, NY New Rochelle, NY Spring 1772 to Boston

A=Francis Asbury 1771-1777:Balt./NJ NYC, Norfolk; Hiding During War in DE, 1778

P = Pilmore mostly in Phil. 1769-1771. Travels South 5/1772-6/1773

W = Robert Williams 1769 NYC, Westchester, NY Phil./Maryland 1772 Norfolk, VA 1773 Petersburg,VA Brunswick Circ. Roanoke River into NC.

K = John King 1769 Phil. Wilmington, DE Maryland, 1st sermon Balt. 1773: NJ 1774: Norfolk 1775: Trenton, NJ 1777: NC circuit

R=Thomas Rankin, 1773-1777: NYC/ Phil.

S=Shadford 1773-1777: Phil./NY Balt. 1775-1776 revival Brunswick circ.

British Methodist Circuit No. 50

Black= Wesley's Missionaries: B, P, A, R, S

Black= Preachers Without License From Wesley: W K

	1773	1774	1775	1776	1777
Total Membership	1,160	2,073	3,148	4,921	6,968
☐ Preachers	10	17	19	24	36
☐ Circuits	6	10	11	15	13

An American Revolution

The Birth of the Methodist Episcopal Church in America

The Revolutionary War from 1775 to 1783 and the newly won independence of the American colonies presented obstacles for American Methodism. After the war, the middle colonies—hardest hit by the war—would never again be the movement's center. Dependent upon Anglican authority for sacramental services, the war forced a reassessment of American Methodists' relationship with the loyalist Church of England, which was largely discredited. As itinerants were free to move about the country, Methodist strength shifted from Philadelphia and New York City into Maryland and points further south in Virginia and North Carolina, where the Anglicans had been strong. The Methodist penchant for pacifism, along with Wesley's public attacks on the patriot movement—most notoriously made in his *Calm Address to the Colonies*—meant that the movement remained in a politically precarious situation requiring real commitment to the new nation and a distancing from the Church of England.

American Methodism had only narrowly avoided a schism in 1779 between northern and southern preachers over the southern preachers' desire to celebrate sacraments—mainly for fear of losing new converts to other churches. Asbury appealed for patience and unity, in the hopes that Wesley would send ordained preachers as the rebellion was nearing its conclusion. After the Revolutionary War concluded in 1783, Methodism in America emerged as a movement of native-born American preachers (all, that is, except their unquestioned leader, Asbury). The movement had grown most in the South where the Church of England had been strong. Having been symbiotically linked to the Church of England's parishes, however, the conclusion of the war left the established church in the middle and southern colonies seriously weakened and in some cases absent. The native-born preachers and Asbury faced the need to stand on their own as a truly American independent church in the newly formed independent nation. Thus the American Revolution stimulated both American Methodists and John Wesley to explore ways to secure ordination. Wesley argued that the development of the episcopal office in the early church was based on the need of oversight and nurture to serve the mission of the church in a region. The episcopacy was not a separate order from elders but rather evolved as a separate office for mission. Therefore, since he had oversight for the mission of Methodism in the New World where no Anglican bishops held authority, Wesley claimed his right as a presbyter to consecrate Thomas Coke as General Superintendent—and to ordain Asbury and consecrate him to that office as well. He also ordained preachers Thomas Vasey and Richard Whatcoat for America. Falling short of naming Coke and Asbury bishops, Wesley did not intend for ordination to lead to separation. Nor did he regard Coke and Asbury's orders as warrant to elevate themselves from mission overseers under Wesley's authority to bishops of an independent church.

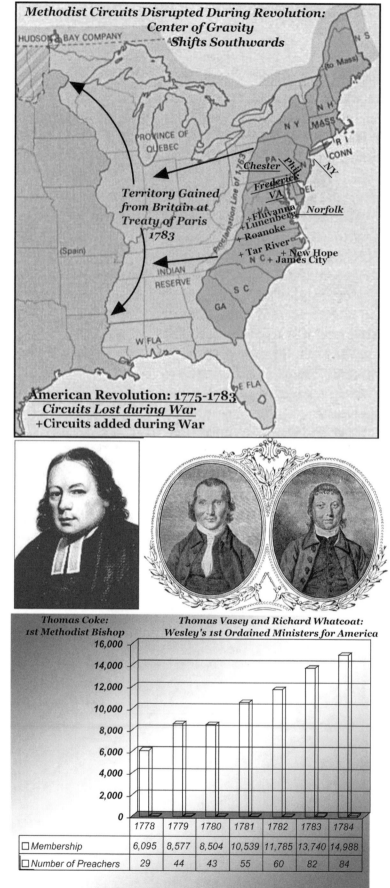

Methodist Circuits Disrupted During Revolution: Center of Gravity Shifts Southwards

HUDSON BAY COMPANY

PROVINCE OF QUEBEC

Territory Gained from Britain at Treaty of Paris 1783

(Spain)

INDIAN RESERVE

Chester

Frederick VA

+Fluvanna
+Lunenberg
+Roanoke
+Tar River
+ New Hope
+ James City
Norfolk

American Revolution: 1775-1783
Circuits Lost during War
+Circuits added during War

Thomas Coke: 1st Methodist Bishop

Thomas Vasey and Richard Whatcoat: Wesley's 1st Ordained Ministers for America

	1778	1779	1780	1781	1782	1783	1784
☐ Membership	6,095	8,577	8,504	10,539	11,785	13,740	14,988
☐ Number of Preachers	29	44	43	55	60	82	84

Something Old, Something New

The Marriage of Methodism and America, 1784

Plans for the founding of an independent church unfolded when Thomas Coke met Asbury and a company of preachers at Barratt's Chapel, near Frederica, Delaware (1). There the first formal Methodist celebration of the Eucharist took place in the New World. The decision was reached to meet at Baltimore to ordain Asbury, Richard Whatcoat, and Thomas Vasey, while also consecrating Asbury as superintendent. Asbury recognized the need to have the American preachers ratify his leadership through a vote, lest the perception remain that the church was being led by Wesley's authority exercised through Coke. In the new Republic, democracy needed to be expressed through the structures of any church that claimed to be American. Freeborn Garrettson and Harry Hosier rode over twelve hundred miles in six weeks calling all Methodist preachers to Baltimore (2). Over sixty preachers arrived at the Lovely Lane Chapel (3) for the conference that ran in late December 1784. In what must be the fastest rise through the ranks of deacon, elder, and superintendent on three consecutive days, Asbury was consecrated bishop through the laying on of hands by Coke and friend Philip Otterbein of Baltimore, who would ultimately form the Methodist-influenced, pietist German revival denomination, the United Brethren. Through the Christmas Conference, the birth of a nation and the birth of sacramental authority in the newly formed Methodist Episcopal Church in America converged. Old doctrinal standards were adopted (Wesley's Sermons), while new authorities adapted (abridgement of Thirty-nine Articles to twenty-five articles with loyalty to America). If the Christmas Conference was a marriage of Methodism and America, it would require a number of years of living into the marriage for the new MEC to truly own its "last name"—America. Indeed, the American Methodist Church was not truly free from suspicion of British loyalties and authority until Thomas Coke was finally marginalized by Asbury and he made his last episcopal visit in 1804. One other sticking point initially put Methodism out of step with the young nation: despite a potentially huge southern and southwestern white membership, many of the American itinerants were active opponents of slavery. Asbury and Coke, particularly, preached emancipation of slaves for Methodist preachers and laity alike, and the first *Discipline* of 1785 explicitly prohibited slavery, stipulating various periods in which slaves must be emancipated. Yet already by the 1790s this stance explicitly against slavery had been noticeably weakened even among the preachers, particularly as the church grew further in Virginia and toward the Deep South. The capitulation to slavery was often subtle, yet the MEC in America could not forever repress its Wesleyan heritage of antislavery. Despite the claims of eyewitnesses that the Christmas Conference was the warm ideal of harmonious Wesleyan conferencing, such a golden age of Methodist unity, if it existed at all, certainly did not last long.

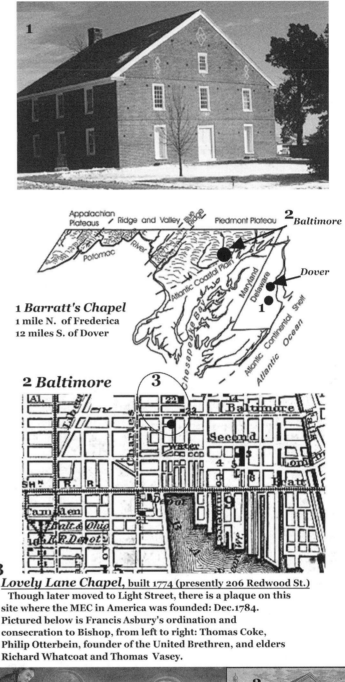

1 *Barratt's Chapel*
1 mile N. of Frederica
12 miles S. of Dover

2 Baltimore

3
Lovely Lane Chapel, built 1774 (presently 206 Redwood St.)
Though later moved to Light Street, there is a plaque on this site where the MEC in America was founded: Dec.1784. Pictured below is Francis Asbury's ordination and consecration to Bishop, from left to right: Thomas Coke, Philip Otterbein, founder of the United Brethren, and elders Richard Whatcoat and Thomas Vasey.

The Prophet of the Long Road and Winding River

Francis Asbury, Mission, and the Mapping of America

Despite many obstacles of geography, religious indifference, bad roads, adverse weather, and little communication, Methodist itinerant missionaries continued to expand their networks throughout the United States. Towering above these many circuit riders and preachers stood Francis Asbury. Asbury was the preeminent itinerant preacher and episcopal networker throughout his forty-six-year ministry from 1771 to 1816. His career can be divided into two phases. The first phase was 1771 to 1784, when Asbury preached more in cities and larger settlements among the colonies. Sometimes as superintendent, and sometimes relieved of that authority, Asbury made it a point to challenge his fellow preachers to keep moving from "the center to the circumference" of each circuit. Yet he was often found preaching during this period across a smaller concentrated region, with longer attention to nurturing the many societies he either found, or had founded himself. The second part of his career—as bishop after his consecration in 1784—saw Asbury's travels driven more by his need to preside over conferences. He also traveled to consolidate and divide circuits to more effectively send preachers into a region and reach a greater saturation density for the Methodist message by meeting in more societies. Thus Asbury preached more briefly over wider distances after 1784.

Asbury was truly free to roam about the country only after the conclusion of the Revolutionary War. Methodists, like all colonists, had been confined east of the Appalachian Mountains by the Line of Proclamation in 1763. Yet with the signing of the Treaty of Paris in 1783, the United States territory expanded to the Mississippi River; and settlers quickly surged westward. Asbury's strategy as bishop was to immediately send circuit riders after the settlers, down the turnpikes, trails, and rivers linking the former colonies with the new frontiers. By quickly following the settlers off the trails up to their fledgling homesteads, Methodists literally knew how to find the lost and lonely swallowed up by the vast country. He instructed circuit riders to arrive so nearly with the first settlers as to essentially make the Methodist circuits into the connecting center of many isolated communities. Asbury desired the sound of the gospel to immediately follow the sound of the first trees falling in an area. To achieve this rapid dispersion, Asbury favored admitting young, single preachers into conference itinerancy. One writer noted that, after the Revolution, only Satan stood between Methodism and the Pacific Ocean. Asbury would have added, only Satan and his preacher's marriages. By visiting circuits early and often, Asbury linked the preachers and their people not only to Methodism but to the entire nation. Because of this strategy, his name became famous. Letters addressed to him from Britain simply as "Francis Asbury, America" were often delivered, as news of his visits traveled fast in most areas. His fame as a traveler across the Appalachians attracted the attention of the US government, who consulted with Asbury about mapping vast areas of frontier settlements. Asbury kept the wheel of itineration rolling quickly down the rivers and roads of America, which he, and his horse, came to know so well they needed neither maps nor guidance. By 1816 at Asbury's death, Methodist circuit riders had put in place the foundation of an evangelical empire consisting of almost 227,000 members, extending from the Atlantic seaboard to the Ohio River Valley and from New England to Natchez.

Asbury's Preaching: by Colony and State

1771=Year of His First Visit
1790=Year of Statehood
(If not Original Colony)

MD=Heart of Asbury's Ministry

1803   1798

NY 1771   1791

CT-RI-Mass.

N.W. Territory   1784 PA 1771   1771
1808   OH 1803
IN 1816   1803   1776*   1776   New Jersey
1790   VA   Delaware
KY 1792   Maryland
1790   1780 NC
TN 1796

** Asbury makes first trip of any American Bishop beyond Appalachian Mountains at Redstone circuit

1785
GA   SC
1789

Note: Asbury was preceded by other preachers into every colony and territory.
Source: Asbury's Journal

*WV part of VA until 1863

Asbury By the Numbers:
At his death in 1816....
Membership:227,000
Miles Travelled:270,000
(1 member for every 1.25 miles travelled)
Sermons preached:16,500
Conferences presided:270
Ordinations: 4,000 Travelled South 30 times over 31 years. By 1811, circled the continent 36 times

Membership Growth from Christmas Conference to Asbury's Death:1785-1816

*Note: the 1817 report of 227,000 reflects membership at Asbury's death

Number of Itinerant Preachers in reports from available years

Every Day Is a Winding Road

Asbury's Rounds and Responsibilities, 1784–1816

Francis Asbury rode his horse an average of 6,000 miles a year overseeing his circuits and conferences. Making his home base in Baltimore, on the dividing line between north and south, Asbury had the choice of striking out in either direction. Like a present-day airline hub, Baltimore was a place through which most of the few good roads leading to population centers in America converged. According to J. Manning Potts, Asbury's travels followed a fairly regular path year to year, with options dictated by the needs of the conferences for espiscopal oversight and appointments.

If Asbury chose to begin his year's travels northward, the round went something like this: Baltimore, Delaware, New Jersey, New York, and up into New England to meet the conference there. Sometimes he would venture as far as Canada. He would circulate around New England usually in the following order: Connecticut, Vermont, New Hampshire, Maine, Massachusetts, Rhode Island, and back through Connecticut to New York (sometimes in reverse). Once in New York again, Asbury would hasten southward: cross New Jersey again, and fan out south and west through southern Pennsylvania, then slip into present-day West Virginia (then still Virginia). Asbury could then take a barge down the Ohio River and preach in its Valley basin on either side—in Ohio (Northwest Territory) and in Kentucky. This river route became the first great westward "highway" for Americans and Methodists, as Asbury pressed his preachers to follow the river exodus. Once in Kentucky, he could preach southward across the rolling plains of Kentucky arriving in Tennessee often through Nashville and the Cumberland River system or cutting closer into Holston River country and the mountains of East Tennessee and western North Carolina through Daniel Boone's famed Cumberland Gap. Once into the Holston area, Asbury could either go south toward Knoxville on the Holston River as it became the headwaters of the Tennessee River, or cut back east through some of the gaps clawed by the westward flows of the connecting French Broad and Nolichucky Rivers to western North Carolina. Either going south to Rutherford or taking the Wilderness Road eastward over to Charlottes Burg (present-day Charlotte), it was then easy to drop down into the South Carolina uplands and over to Augusta to meet the Georgia Conference often held in Washington Wilkes, along the Broad River and the Savannah River. Although Asbury held no fond feelings for them due to their plantation gaiety, Asbury would reluctantly enter Savannah and quickly make a pass northward through Charles Town (Charleston). From here he could take either the coastline Post Road or the middle route (Western Road) back through North Carolina into Virginia, meeting the conferences often at Petersburg or one of the other larger Tidewater towns. From there a trip to Washington was easy, concluding the year with the short trip "home" to Baltimore. Then he would rest for Christmas and begin the trek again, sometimes reversing it. If home is where the heart is, then for Asbury he was at home wherever his heart and his feet (and his praying knees) met God's earth.

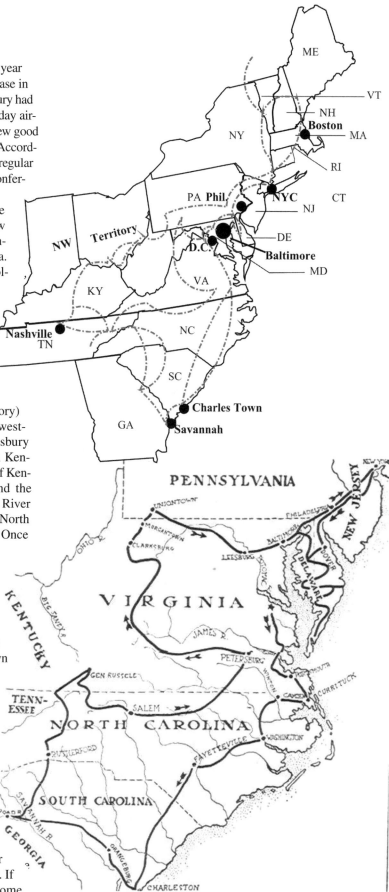

Asbury's Preaching and Episcopal Journey for 1788

Over the River and through the Woods

Asbury Oversees Growing Circuits and Expanding Conferences

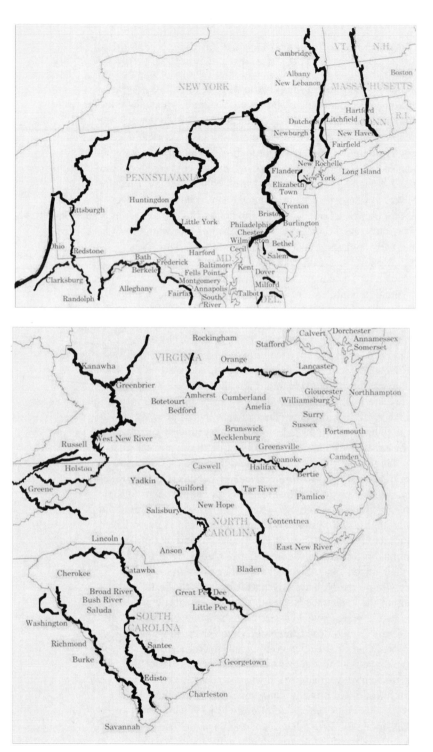

Like the Roman roads of old, the dusty paths and rivers the circuit riders rode were the channels along which the Methodists built a connectional church. Where Methodism entered territories before states were formed (in all but seven cases), the names of rivers were often chosen for the circuit name, secondarily county names—which were only developing in the east when Methodism was expanding. Methodism, thereby, not only reformed the nation, but in so doing, formed and sometimes even named the nation through a vast network of circuits. In 1796, the first set of geographically linked conferences was established, which in many cases only grouped unique river and road communities together in a tenuous, foreign construct driven by a state name. There were initially six Conferences fixed along state lines, overseen on an annual basis: Baltimore, Virginia, Philadelphia, South Carolina, New England, and the Western Conference. (By 1800 these had grown to seven, and by 1820, eleven Conferences.) A common identity for settlers was slow to dawn, with larger cultural linkages often won through the hard work of circuit riders across difficult passages that divided most small-scale communities. This was even more marked for those first circuits beyond the Appalachians.

From the origins of American Methodism at the Christmas Conference to the time immediately after Asbury's death, the sheer increase in the number of circuits is striking. In 1784, at the formation of the Methodist Episcopal Church in America, there were a total of 46 circuits in Methodism, most of them centered around Baltimore and southward toward Virginia—mainly because Baltimore was the early "hub" of America with all the earliest major roads running through it. In 1790, depicted in our map, there were already 100 circuits. By 1819, three years after Asbury's death, there were 475 circuits. Methodism had by that time penetrated only from its earliest colonial heartlands on the coast as far west and south as the following areas that later became states: Ohio, Indiana, Missouri, Kentucky, Tennessee, Alabama, Mississippi, and Louisiana. Even in these frontier territories, Methodism was neither firmly nor densely established. Yet in 1819, 475 circuits constituted a tenfold increase in number of circuits without a correspon-

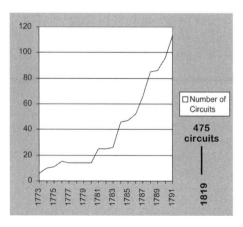

ding tenfold increase in area. Methodism may have in cases "civilized" the frontiers, but it grew east of the Mississippi primarily because it focused its efforts on nurturing the emergent middle class agrarian settlements. Eccentric heroes often got the attention for exploring new vistas, but Methodism would grow with the country because it would go with the country: that is, it would grow by focusing on the demographic movements and settlement patterns capable of supporting a growing church infrastructure. As the frontiers east of the Mississippi receded into stable settlements, itinerancy meant that laity, local class leaders, and Methodist preachers were together in place to connect various locations and institutions across the developing American landscape. Methodist itinerant polity was better adapted to initiating and sustaining work among newly emerging settlements, and somewhat less inclined to launching new work far beyond the "frontiers" of demographic growth. Methodist movements were much more effective at consolidating their work through the division of circuits among growing population groups—than is generally held in popular conceptions.

Teach Your Children Well

The Rise and Spread of Methodist Higher Education

John and Charles Wesley clearly held strong convictions about higher education serving faith. Indeed, in the hymn "Come, Father, Son, and Holy Ghost," Charles affirmed, "Unite the pair so disjoin'd, knowledge and vital piety." But American Methodists have struggled to see these connections early and often. The stillborn effort of Thomas Coke and Francis Asbury to found Cokesbury College (1787) in Maryland surely gave pause to those Methodists inclined to found colleges. Moreover, Methodism's rapid spread across the frontier using the circuit rider and camp meeting preaching dampened enthusiasm and demand for colleges. Famous circuit riders such as Alfred Brunson and Peter Cartwright claimed that education was worthless to a pastor, who simply needed to get a good horse, have a seasoned mentor, and hit the circuits—often called the "Bush College." Yet as Methodism grew wealthier along with the country from the 1820s, a number of changes promoted higher education. As the number of station charges increased, and the camp meeting became more stylized, preachers were spending more time and effort in ministry within one local church. The need for a more learned ministry to provide educational variety and stimulating preaching became clear. Calls from the laity for Methodist colleges partly arose from concern for their sons and later daughters to achieve educational advantages not afforded to them. Yet the laity and clergy found common cause to provide education in the Wesleyan spirit even more out of fear—lest the new generation of wealthier Methodists be lost to other denominations with schools. Sunday schools became attractive, and graded curriculum was developed from the late 1820s, but was not enough to satisfy the lay hunger for knowledge. Academies, or secondary schools, came first, often with mixed success due to funding shortfalls. The General Conference of 1820 directed annual conferences to build colleges. Then an explosion of college building swept the MEC across the north, and to a lesser degree, the south.

The church continued to employ the course of study to educate its pastors, remaining resistant to theological education into the late 1850s. Yet with a new generation of educated men and women taking their place leading the churches, a renewed call for theological education began to garner attention, for fear that graduates would not continue to attend worship led by unlearned pastors. Fear of losing this generation, plus the rise of Methodist international mission prompted Bishop Randolph Foster and missionary secretary John P. Durbin to articulate the need for theological seminaries. Their arguments found official backing at the 1856 General Conference of the MEC, and a number of institutions were consequently founded. The number of seminaries founded picked up momentum throughout the late nineteenth and early twentieth centuries. Yet even with this new commitment to theological education, the course of study continued to be the primary entry gate into ministry as late as the 1950s. Indeed, a graduate theological degree only became mandated for elder's orders by decision of the General Conference of 1956. Each era must rethink the education required for ministry. But if we wish to speak with confidence through our faith to an increasingly complex world, we should be slow to drive a wedge between knowledge and piety.

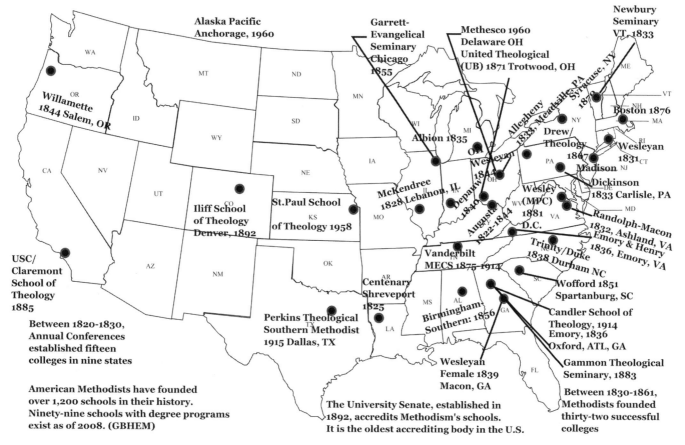

Of Barns and Brethren

The Origins and Expansion of the United Brethren, 1767–1968

If the MEC in America traces its foundation from card games to classes, then the United Brethren has an equally impressive story arc: from Barns to Brethren to Bishops, the German-American United Brethren ultimately put the "U" in the United Methodist Church merger of 1968. This antecedent denomination of United Methodism is often accorded status as the first denomination formed completely on North American soil. Its roots lay in the late-eighteenth-century revival that touched most of the denominations of recent German immigrants to America, particularly in the colonies of Pennsylvania, Maryland, and northern Virginia. In 1767, a German Reformed Church missionary to America named Philip William Otterbein (1) experienced an evangelical awakening while serving in Lancaster, Pennsylvania. He began to visit the numerous revival meetings held in the barns of German American farmers, called in German "Gross Versammlungen"—or Great Meetings. Visiting one of these meetings in Isaac Long's barn (3) north of Lancaster, Pennsylvania, Otterbein became deeply moved and impressed with the Mennonite lay preacher Martin Boehm's (2) message of vital and personal religious devotion. Otterbein greeted Boehm at the end of the service with the words, "Wir sind Brüdern"—"We are brothers"— from which the denomination would ultimately take its name. At first Otterbein and Boehm preached in numerous Great Meetings to the various immigrants to stimulate pietistic renewal without a thought given to forming a new denomination. By the early 1770s, Otterbein's work had gathered attention from various awakened German immigrants, touching many Mennonite, Amish, Moravian, and Lutheran congregations. Invited to serve the German Reformed Church in Baltimore in 1774, Otterbein befriended Francis Asbury and they became lifelong admirers, co-evangelists, and friends. Present at Asbury's ordination and consecration as bishop, Otterbein and his "Brethren" found even more brothers among the Methodists and shared their pietistic, heart-warmed evangelical message. Otterbein remained a pastor in the independent German Reformed Church in Baltimore until he died, but he enjoyed a freedom to preach widely to German immigrants along with Asbury, which led ultimately to a meeting at Peter Kemp's farmhouse (4) at Frederick, Maryland, in September, 1800. At this meeting, a fellowship of preachers participating in Otterbein's evangelistic outreach decided to band together into a formal company of "nonsectarian" preachers meeting yearly in conference. This group elected Otterbein and Boehm as the first two bishops of the new Christian renewal movement known as "die Vereinigten Brüdern" (United Brethren). Martin Boehm and Otterbein both worked closely with the Methodists and particularly Asbury, often preaching in combined meetings for Methodists and Brethren alike. Boehm even was a member of a Methodist class at one time, and his son Henry Boehm became a traveling Methodist preacher who often accompanied Asbury on itinerant preaching tours as preacher and translator for the Germans. The closeness of the preaching and the polity of the Brethren and the Methodists led many in Pennsylvania to call the UB somewhat erroneously the "Dutch Methodists."

After Boehm died (March 1812), the Brethren elected lay preacher Christian Newcomer to the espiscopacy. Otterbein died soon after, in November 1813. At the first General Conference in 1815, rules of discipline were drawn up; and from this point the movement was no longer an extension of its founders. Newcomer patterned the church more strongly after the Methodists by adopting much from the *Discipline*. Newcomer also spearheaded the early westward march of the United Brethren as they followed German immigrants to Ohio, Indiana, Illinois, and to many other parts of the country. When Newcomer died in 1830, the United Brethren comprised between fifteen to twenty thousand members. In the late 1880s, Bishop Milton Wright (father of the famed flying Wright Brothers) led a group that wanted to maintain the Old Constitution, and they separated from those who wanted to invoke change (New Constitution). Descendants of the Old Constitution continue to exist today. In 1946 at Johnstown, Pennsylvania, the Evangelical United Brethren was formed through the union of the UB (New Constitution) with the Evangelical Association. As ethnic distinctives waned in the postwar era, the way was clear for mergers to reclaim a common Wesleyan-Arminian heritage. At the formation of The United Methodist Church in 1968, the common heritage of the United Brethren, the Evangelical Church, and Methodism was formally claimed.

Philip William Otterbein (1726-1813)

1

Martin Boehm (1725-1812)

2

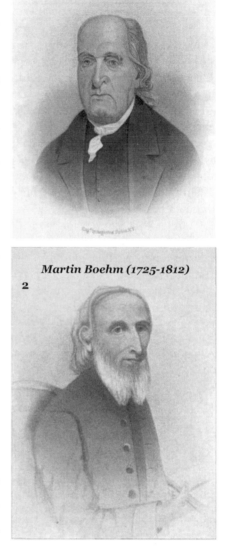

Isaac Long's Barn, Lancaster, PA

3

Peter Kemp's House, Frederick, MD

4

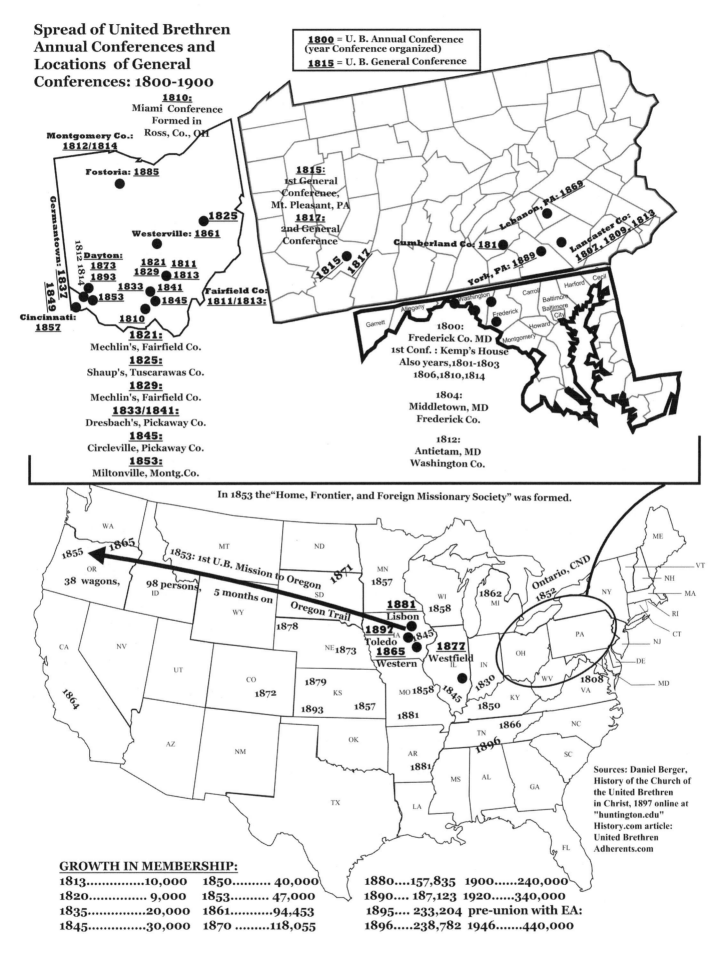

Spread of United Brethren Annual Conferences and Locations of General Conferences: 1800-1900

1800 = U. B. Annual Conference (year Conference organized)
1815 = U. B. General Conference

1810:
Miami Conference Formed in Ross, Co., OH

Montgomery Co.: **1812/1814**

Fostoria: **1885**

Germantown: **1812 1814 1837 1849**

1825

Westerville: **1861**

Dayton:
1873
1893

1821 1811
1829 1813

1833 1841
1853 1845

1810

Cincinnati: **1857**

Fairfield Co: **1811/1813:**

1821:
Mechlin's, Fairfield Co.
1825:
Shaup's, Tuscarawas Co.
1829:
Mechlin's, Fairfield Co.
1833/1841:
Dresbach's, Pickaway Co.
1845:
Circleville, Pickaway Co.
1853:
Miltonville, Montg. Co.

1815:
1st General Conference, Mt. Pleasant, PA
1817:
2nd General Conference

1815 1817

Cumberland Co.: **181**

Lebanon, PA: **1869**

Lancaster Co: **1807, 1809, 1813**

York, PA: **1889**

Garrett — Allegany — Washington — Frederick — Carroll — Baltimore — Baltimore City — Harford — Cecil — Howard — Montgomery

1800:
Frederick Co. MD
1st Conf. : Kemp's House
Also years, 1801-1803
1806, 1810, 1814

1804:
Middletown, MD
Frederick Co.

1812:
Antietam, MD
Washington Co.

In 1853 the "Home, Frontier, and Foreign Missionary Society" was formed.

WA
1865
1855
OR
38 wagons,
1853: 1st U.B. Mission to Oregon
98 persons,
5 months on
Oregon Trail
ID
1878

MT
ND
1871
MN
1857
SD
WY
NE **1873**

CA
NV
UT
CO
1872
KS
1879
1893
1857

AZ
NM

1881
Lisbon
1897
IA **1845**
Toledo
1865
Western
MO **1858**

1877
Westfield
IL
1845
IN **1830**
KY **1850**

WI
1858
MI **1862**

Ontario, CND
1852

OH
WV
1808
VA

PA
NY
VT
NH
MA
RI
CT
NJ
DE
MD
ME

TN
1866
1896
NC
SC

AR
1881
MS
AL
GA

TX
LA
FL

Sources: Daniel Berger, History of the Church of the United Brethren in Christ, 1897 online at "huntington.edu" History.com article: United Brethren Adherents.com

GROWTH IN MEMBERSHIP:

1813	10,000	1850	40,000
1820	9,000	1853	47,000
1835	20,000	1861	94,453
1845	30,000	1870	118,055

1880	157,835	1900	240,000
1890	187,123	1920	340,000
1895	233,204	pre-union with EA:
1896	238,782	1946	440,000

Farming Out the Faith

Jacob Albright and the Rise of the Evangelical Association

Intersecting with both the MEC in America and the United Brethren was another pietistic denomination based among the German immigrant population in late eighteenth-century America: the Evangelical Association. In ways similar to the United Brethren, the Evangelical Association (EA) took shape under the influence of Methodism and ultimately found its way full circle back to Methodism. Founded by farmer Jacob Albrecht (or Albright) in Lancaster County, Pennsylvania, the Evangelical Association grew to be an independent denomination over a shorter time span than the earlier German church renewal group, the United Brethren. A nominal Lutheran, after the death of some of his children Albright found comfort from a neighboring farmer associated with the United Brethren, as well as a local Methodist lay preacher-farmer in the area. He joined a Methodist class meeting, adopted a rigid asceticism, and in 1796 began to preach the Methodist message of personal holiness as evidence of faith. Seeking to find an organization to nurture the many German-speaking converts he was reaching, Albright created three Methodist-inspired classes in southeastern Pennsylvania in 1800. Numerous lay preachers were developed through these classes. In fact, the classes had already produced enough lay preachers to form a network of itinerants preaching the evangelical faith throughout eastern Pennsylvania and northern Virginia. Thus in November 1803, Albright met with other German preachers to provide coordination for their work, and the formal founding of the Evangelical Association is traced to this meeting. Here Albright was elected as an elder and supervisor of the other preachers, receiving a license and ordination from two of the lay preachers. After the first annual conference in 1807, Albright was elected a bishop of the movement that was known at the time as "The Newly-Formed Methodist Conference," but he died six months later of tuberculosis in March 1808. The preachers resisted using the term *church* and only took the name "Evangelische Gemeinschaft" (Evangelical Association) at the first General Conference in 1816 in New Berlin, Pennsylvania.

Two successors made important contributions to the shape and growth of the movement. Elder George Miller adapted Methodist theology and polity to create Articles of Faith and the first *Discipline* for the EA in 1809. Oversight was lodged in the role of the presiding elder, and no other bishops were elected until John Seybert became the second bishop in 1839. His work was the stimulus for the expansion of the Evangelical Association among the numerous German populations that immigrated to America beginning in the 1840s. Seybert, a lifelong bachelor, focused on itinerating among the Germans from Ohio to the Great Plains, with somewhat lesser attention to the Germans in the east. His episcopal travels took him from Pennsylvania to the Rocky Mountains, and even into Canada—traveling an estimated 175,000 miles and showing remarkable similarities to Francis Asbury.

As the EA constituency spread out into new regions and had different experiences with other churches, theological tensions emerged around entire sanctification in the late eighteenth century. This culminated in a bitter split between the more traditional Wesleyan EA and those seeking a more Reformed sanctification theology—which formed into the United Evangelical Church at Naperville, Illinois, in 1894. The two groups reunited in 1922 as the Evangelical Church. Unification talks began in 1932 between the EC and the United Brethren. After WWII, the groups completed their union, forming the Evangelical United Brethren Church in Johnstown, Pennsylvania, in 1946. Yet with the sharp loss of identification with their German heritage, the EUB faced an uncertain future. With German identity no longer at stake, the EUB entered talks with The Methodist Church in the 1950s to reunite churches with common origins, theology, and polity. The United Methodist Church was formed in Dallas, Texas, in 1968. The use of the word *United* in the UMC was chosen to signify the combined EUB heritage brought into the merger. The name *Evangelical Methodist Church* was only narrowly outvoted. Clearly the loss of the term *Evangelical* made the Evangelical Association heritage less visible in the new denomination. Nevertheless, as Albright's people moved from farms to "farming out" their faith across the nation, the one-time Newly-Formed Methodist Connection ironically, once again, stimulated a newly formed United Methodist Church.

Jacob Albrecht (Albright)
Founder and First Bishop
of the Evangelical Association, 1807

Johannes (John) Seybert
elected second bishop of
the Evangelical Association, 1839

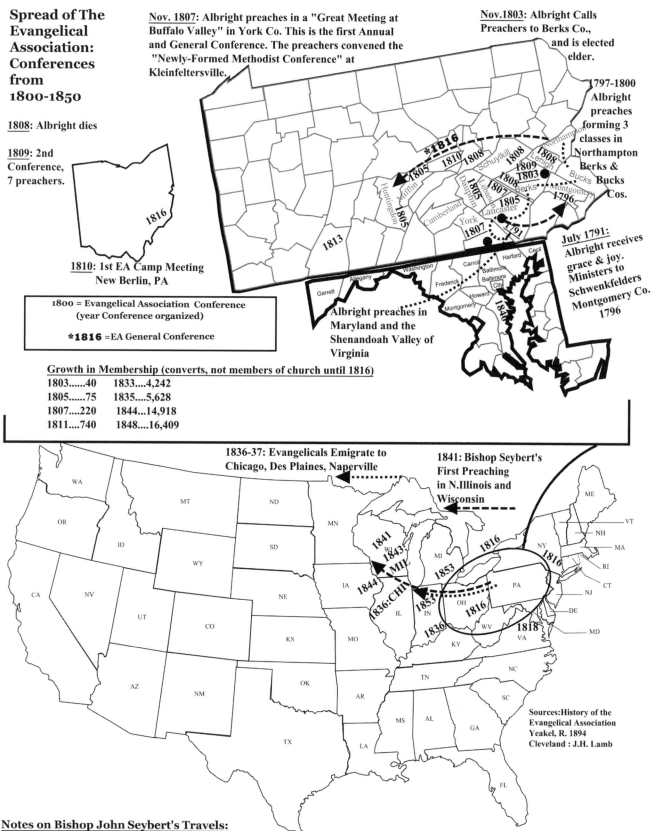

Spread of The Evangelical Association: Conferences from 1800-1850

Nov. 1807: Albright preaches in a "Great Meeting at Buffalo Valley" in York Co. This is the first Annual and General Conference. The preachers convened the "Newly-Formed Methodist Conference" at Kleinfeltersville.

Nov.1803: Albright Calls Preachers to Berks Co., and is elected elder.

1797-1800 Albright preaches forming 3 classes in Northampton Berks & Bucks Cos.

1808: Albright dies

1809: 2nd Conference, 7 preachers.

1810: 1st EA Camp Meeting New Berlin, PA

1800 = Evangelical Association Conference (year Conference organized)

***1816** =EA General Conference

July 1791: Albright receives grace & joy. Ministers to Schwenkfelders Montgomery Co. 1796

Albright preaches in Maryland and the Shenandoah Valley of Virginia

Growth in Membership (converts, not members of church until 1816)

1803......40	1833....4,242
1805......75	1835....5,628
1807....220	1844...14,918
1811....740	1848...16,409

1836-37: Evangelicals Emigrate to Chicago, Des Plaines, Naperville

1841: Bishop Seybert's First Preaching in N.Illinois and Wisconsin

Sources:History of the Evangelical Association Yeakel, R. 1894 Cleveland : J.H. Lamb

Notes on Bishop John Seybert's Travels:

In 1825 Seybert was appointed to the Canaan District in Pennsylvania (a large area mostly east of the Susquehanna River, south into Virginia, and into New York). After his election as Bishop in 1839, his preaching and supervising took him repeatedly from New York, to New Jersey, through Ohio and Pennsylvania, Maryland, the Shenandoah Valley, as far west as St. Louis, Indiana, eastern Iowa, northern Illinois, Milwaukee, Detroit, and Canada.

"Nothing but Crows and Methodist Preachers"

Circuits Connect the Nation to the Mississippi River by 1830

"The weather is so bad, there's nothing out but crows and Methodist preachers."

Nineteenth-century American folk saying

Methodism could grow with the nation, because it would go with the nation. Methodism rapidly spread along the rivers and roads westward, accompanying the thrust of population movements in the early nineteenth century. Only the US Postal Service had more branches and coverage than Methodist churches—the country's first great private franchise. Yet, Methodism, far from being unified, found itself torn early and regularly by regional schisms—precisely because its rapid growth made the church trans-regional. Schisms in 1792 (O'Kelly Schism), 1830 (Methodist Protestant Church), 1842 (the Wesleyans), 1845 (Northern and Southern halves), and 1860 (Free Methodists) bear testimony to how regional and cultural politics, along with the rising wealth in the 1820s of the Methodist church in the agrarian settlements of the East, often drove the practice and polity of Methodist mission. In both practical and theological terms, each schism compromised the hard work and high ideals of a connectional, national Methodist witness. Nevertheless, by the eve of the Civil War, the various branches of Methodism accounted for an estimated one-third of American church membership; they boasted close to twenty thousand places of worship, eight thousand more than the Baptists, their closest competitors.

The power of the circuit-riding system to spread the message of holy living in widely scattered communities over a vast continent was clear. Circuit riders traveled light through heavy weather to penetrate the margins of emerging settlements. But the emphasis on movement was not the entire story. The ability to create so many more places of worship than their competitors without many educated or ordained clergy or large investment of capital, multiplied and amplified the centers where the egalitarian Wesleyan message could be preached and practiced. This growth was possible because of the steady commitments of the lay, local class leaders. With a complementary structure, the circuit riders could move from the center to the circumference to preach the broad themes of the Wesleyan message. It fell to the local class leaders to do the hard work of nurture across the seasons of a community's life, with all the highs and lows of living with the ironic combination of vulnerability to isolation along with intense personal and communal relations. The circuit rider and the class leader were true explorers, partners in a dance across the widest landscapes of the nation and into the deepest interior landscapes of spirit and personality. The two together, each in his own way, connected isolated folks with news and fresh observations, and provided stimulations of various kinds with different rhythms and rituals.

By the 1820s, improved roads and river travel were making travel across the eastern US easier. These

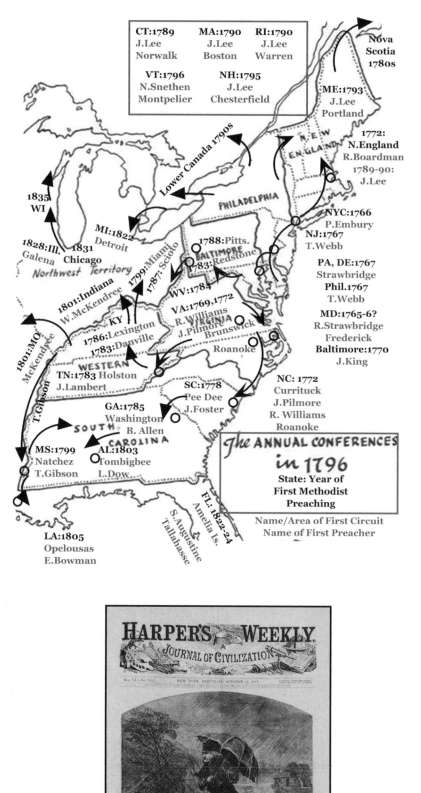

improved conditions allowed more preachers to saturate more areas, promoting and requiring better-organized annual conferences. With more preachers covering smaller conference boundaries, the frequency of contact between preacher and societies increased, improving the nurture opportunities. As camp meetings flourished from 1800 to the 1850s, this further concentrated preaching into closer proximity with population centers. More concentrated preaching allowed regional revival fires to be stoked on a regular basis and meant less distance to the nearest class meeting. The long-term steady growth of Methodism was dependent upon keeping the line tight between conversion at camp meeting and nurture at class meetings. Because circuit riders and class leaders were effective in holding that connection, Methodism, unlike its competitors, could rapidly mount initiatives among marginal population groups (slaves, Native Americans, poor settlers, urban migrants), while consolidating its gains among a nationwide church. Frontier Methodism was effective, at the very least, because it offered a level of pastoral and human care otherwise unavailable in the harsh forests, mountain hollows, and wide grassland (and the growing cities) of the young Republic. Circuit riders maintained proximity to new settlers through presence: living simply and leaving home—all to be on the same roads and rivers traveled by settlers. Under Asbury, Whatcoat, and William McKendree's radical commitment to an itinerating superintendency, Methodist circuit riders not only followed the people along the rivers and roads, but, more importantly, their mobility allowed them to penetrate far beyond the usual pathways dictated by commerce and immigration alone.

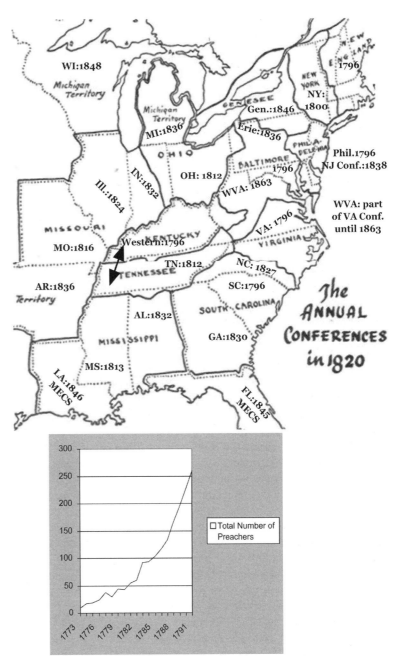

William McKendree was bishop of the MEC from 1808-1835. He oversaw a period of rapid expansion of circuits and the need for administrative structures that could support the growing conferences. As the first native-born Methodist Bishop, McKendree realized with the vast conferences, and the growing populist democratic tone of the country, the Episcopacy needed to be adapted: he delegated powers of appointment more democratically and practically to the input of presiding elders, today's D.S. He was bishop when the delegated General Conference was enacted. The Constitution of Methodism, along with its non-negotiable Restrictive Rules, were formulated while he was Bishop. These measures translated into strengthened Annual Conferences and less autocracy for the Episcopacy. Known as the "Apostle of the West," he oversaw preaching and camp meetings on Methodisms' Western frontier, being the first Bishop to itinerate in Indiana and Missouri. Today, McKendree's Chapel marks the first Methodist chapel built west of the Mississippi, at Cape Girardeau, MO. He died near Nashville, his home for many years, and is buried in the Bishops' cemetery at Vanderbilt School of Divinity.

"Holy Knock 'Em Down Power"

Camp Meetings and Methodist Consolidation of Frontier Religion

The origin of the camp meeting revival is a matter of some disagreement among historians of American religious history. Some suggest that camp meetings occurred as early as 1797 in rural southern Kentucky. But it is clear that James McGready, a Presbyterian preacher of great power, began around 1800 to exhort listeners in Logan County, Kentucky, to seek the "new birth." In one of these religious meetings in July of that year, McGready preached over a four-day period along the Red River in Logan County, producing many transformed lives. The brothers William and John McGee heard McGready's preaching and began to preach farther in the county. A Methodist minister, John McGee, held one of the earliest camp meetings in Tennessee at Drakes' Creek, Sumner County, in August 1800. Other Presbyterians and Methodists held similar meetings on the frontier in the summertime, when the weather was good and the crops were largely harvested. The most famous early camp meeting was held at Cane Ridge in Bourbon County, Kentucky, in August 1801. Estimates vary that from ten thousand to thirty thousand people camped on fields and heard the frenzied preaching from open-air stands. The Cane Ridge event was led by the future founder of the Restorationist Disciples of Christ—Presbyterian preacher Barton Stone. Twenty other ministers preached there at Cane Ridge, including numerous Methodists, and these revivals quickly became a central feature of Methodist life during the Second Great Awakening, from 1800 until the 1840s. The United Brethren and the Evangelical Association also made heavy use of the camp meeting.

Structurally, the camp meeting was held in its earliest period inside a "brush arbor" cleared from a frontier wilderness, centrally located enough to emerging population centers to attract upwards of thousands of participants, often from several denominations. Permanent structures usually replaced tents in the "arbor" as the camp meetings developed over time. People came from a wide area and stayed several nights—often Thursday through Sunday. The crowd—full of both saints and sinners—moved expectantly through the torch-lit campground, hearing an almost continuous sound of emotional preaching and hymnal singing. The combination of dramatic human performance, wider social interaction, and the wilderness setting all inspired intense religious reactions. Extreme religious practices were common early in the development of this revival form, such as violent spasms called the "jerks," loud cries known as "barks," and fainting into deep trances. The eccentric itinerant evangelist Lorenzo Dow claimed that these remarkable spiritual effects were distributed among both men and women, regardless of age, race, and economic level.

The intensity of these religious experiences was certainly supported by the intense social life of the campground. Families would gather together in groups, and social ties based on region or wider kinship ties found reinforcement through eating and living together in a temporary community. These gatherings provided a meeting place for old friends and new ones— and even an opportunity to find suitable marriage partners. The combination of social possibilities on the edge of vulnerability in the wilderness was a potent mix for personal and spiritual awakening. While many participants fell away from the intensity of the spiritual experience once they returned to their homes and joined churches, many maintained ties to the faith they had discovered during these meetings.

William McKendree, bishop of the Western Conference (present-day Tennessee and Kentucky), was perhaps one of the foremost proponents of the camp meeting, along with Francis Asbury late in his career. They both were particularly effective in systematizing the meetings, and connecting them to developing Methodist organizational structures.

Methodist Camp Meeting, March 1, 1819

Lorenzo Dow, 1777-1834

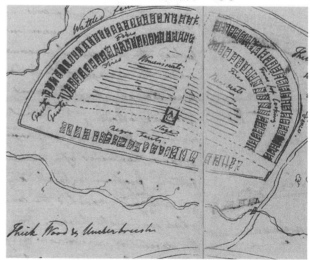

Camp Meeting Plan, 1809, Fairfax Co., VA

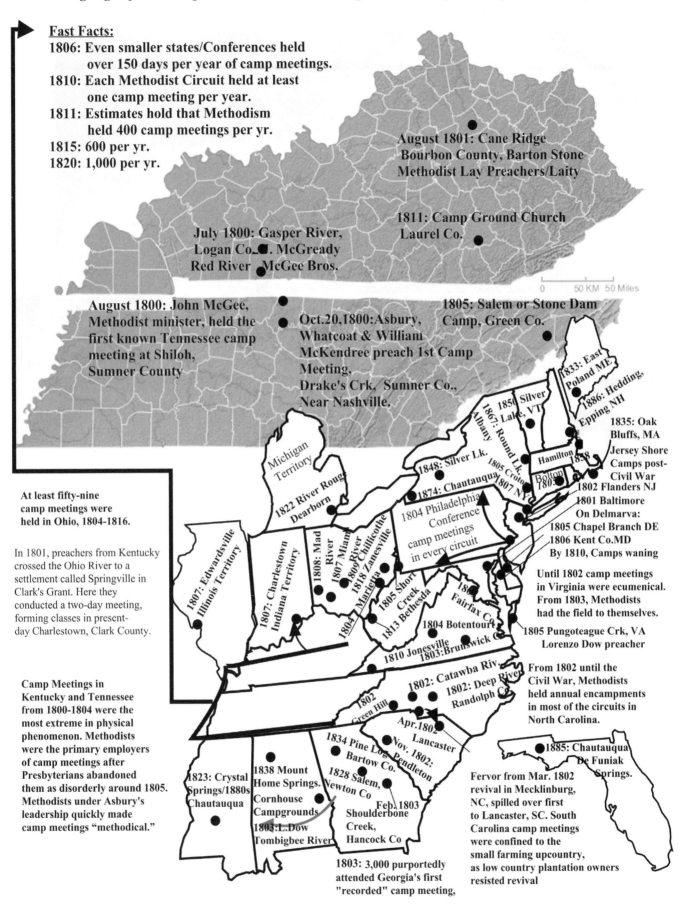

Fast Facts:

1806: Even smaller states/Conferences held over 150 days per year of camp meetings.

1810: Each Methodist Circuit held at least one camp meeting per year.

1811: Estimates hold that Methodism held 400 camp meetings per yr.

1815: 600 per yr.

1820: 1,000 per yr.

August 1801: Cane Ridge Bourbon County, Barton Stone Methodist Lay Preachers/Laity

1811: Camp Ground Church Laurel Co.

July 1800: Gasper River, Logan Co. J. McGready Red River McGee Bros.

August 1800: John McGee, Methodist minister, held the first known Tennessee camp meeting at Shiloh, Sumner County

Oct.20,1800:Asbury, Whatcoat & William McKendree preach 1st Camp Meeting, Drake's Crk, Sumner Co., Near Nashville.

1805: Salem or Stone Dam Camp, Green Co.

0 50 KM 50 Miles

At least fifty-nine camp meetings were held in Ohio, 1804-1816.

In 1801, preachers from Kentucky crossed the Ohio River to a settlement called Springville in Clark's Grant. Here they conducted a two-day meeting, forming classes in present-day Charlestown, Clark County.

Camp Meetings in Kentucky and Tennessee from 1800-1804 were the most extreme in physical phenomenon. Methodists were the primary employers of camp meetings after Presbyterians abandoned them as disorderly around 1805. Methodists under Asbury's leadership quickly made camp meetings "methodical."

1833: East Poland ME
1886: Hedding, Epping NH
1850: Silver Lake, VT
1867: Round Lk.
1805 Croton
Albany
Hamilton 1858
1835: Oak Bluffs, MA
Jersey Shore Camps post-Civil War
1848: Silver Lk.
1874: Chautauqua
1807 NYC
Bolton 1805
1802 Flanders NJ
1801 Baltimore
1804 Philadelphia Conference camp meetings in every circuit
On Delmarva:
1805 Chapel Branch DE
1806 Kent Co.MD
By 1810, Camps waning

Michigan Territory
1822 River Rouge Dearborn

1807: Edwardsville Illinois Territory

1807: Charlestown Indiana Territory

1808: Mad River
1807 Miami River
1809 Chillicothe
1818 Zanesville
1804 Marietta
1805 Short Creek
1813 Bethesda
1804 Fairfax Ct.
1804 Botentourt
1810 Jonesville
1803:Brunswick Co

Until 1802 camp meetings in Virginia were ecumenical. From 1803, Methodists had the field to themselves.

1805 Pungoteague Crk, VA Lorenzo Dow preacher

From 1802 until the Civil War, Methodists held annual encampments in most of the circuits in North Carolina.

1802: Catawba Riv.
1802: Deep River Randolph Co
1802 Green Hill
Apr.1802 Lancaster
Nov. 1802: Pendleton
1834 Pine Log Bartow Co.
1828 Salem, Newton Co
Feb.1803 Shoulderbone Creek, Hancock Co
1823: Crystal Springs/1880s Chautauqua
1838 Mount Home Springs. Cornhouse Campgrounds
1803:L.Dow Tombigbee River
1885: Chautauqua De Funiak Springs.

Fervor from Mar. 1802 revival in Mecklinburg, NC, spilled over first to Lancaster, SC. South Carolina camp meetings were confined to the small farming upcountry, as low country plantation owners resisted revival

1803: 3,000 purportedly attended Georgia's first "recorded" camp meeting,

Balconies, Blacksmiths, and Bishops

Formation and Spread of the African Methodist Episcopal Church

The story of African American Methodism and the earliest chapter of minority rights in American history are inextricably linked to the career of Richard Allen. Born a slave, Allen bought his freedom and then achieved a number of historical milestones: founder of the first African American empowerment group (Freedman's Aid Society, 1787); first African American ordained clergy (1799); and first African American consecrated bishop in America (1816). Converted as a youth, Allen quickly immersed himself in St. George's worship and class meetings in Philadelphia. He became a licensed preacher in 1784, quickly rising to the attention of Asbury. He is thought to have been present at the Christmas Conference. Though Philadelphia consisted of many freedmen, racial tensions remained and were expressed in church seating attitudes. Often made to sit in the balconies or one to a pew against the wall, African American Methodists experienced both subtle and overt discrimination. In 1787, matters came to a head at the divided altar of St. George's. The expectation was that African Americans must wait on attending prayers and Communion at the altar until the whites were served. Yet Richard Allen sought to integrate Communion. He and other black worshipers were pulled off their knees and ordered to the back part of the house or to the balcony. Richard Allen said, "If you will wait until prayers are over, I will bother you no more." He led the African Americans out of St. George's and, through a gradual series of independent actions, gathered a nucleus for worship and preaching under him. Allen still enjoyed the confidence and support of Asbury, receiving full elder's orders while still under episcopal authority (1799). Yet Allen knew his followers could not continue worshiping separately at St. George's.

Allen took some of his earnings and purchased property at Sixth and Lombard Streets in Philadelphia. He then purchased Sim's blacksmith shop and, with his teamster experience, hauled the shop to his land. He converted it to a meeting house in 1794. Asbury was present at the dedication of this historic church, which was named "Bethel," or "house of God." While some blacks joined the Episcopal Church or the small African Union Church, those who wished to remain in the Methodist faith soon gathered about Allen. Growth occurred steadily, yet many of the "Allenites" feared the conference would confiscate the land according to the Model Deed. To address this, Allen initiated a series of expensive lawsuits to prevent the Philadelphia Conference from claiming their property. Victory was gained in the courts, a charter obtained from the General Assembly of Pennsylvania, and the legal foundations for an independent black Methodist church were in place. Through the process, it became clear that under Methodist polity the Allenites would need to be independent to maintain control of their property. Clear on their commitment to Wesleyan theology and polity, Allen invited other marginalized black Methodists to Philadelphia twenty-nine years later in 1816 to found an independent Methodist denomination. There were five churches affiliated with Allen, spread over these northeastern cities at the time. After the founding of the AME, bishops Morris Brown and Daniel Payne led its expansion after the Civil War beyond its concentration in northern urban areas to become a national, Wesleyan, African American Church. Today, the AME is represented in over thirty countries around the globe.

**Bishop Richard Allen
(1760-1831)
Founder/First Bishop**

**Mother Bethel AME, Phil.
erected in1894**

**Bishop Morris Brown
(1770-1849)
Missionary Superintendent
for the South, Mid-west,
and Canada.**

**Bishop Daniel Payne
(1811-1893)
AME Historian and 1st
African American College
President (Wilberforce, OH)**

	1816.	1836.	1866.	1896.	1916.
No. of churches	7	86	286	4,850	7,500
No. of bishops	1	2	3	9	16
No. of conferences	2	4	10	52	81
No. of schools	0	0	1	20	24
No. of ministers	7	27	265	4,365	6,650
No. of local preachers					6,400
No. of members	400	7,594	73,000	518,000	650,000

Twentieth Century Statistics and World Distribution:

	1946	2007
No. of churches	c.5,000	c. 6,200
Inclusive members	c.1,000,000	c. 2,500,000
No. of preachers		8,000
No. of Bishops		20

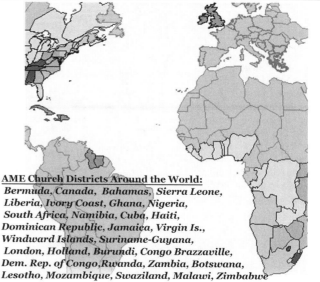

AME Church Districts Around the World:
*Bermuda, Canada, Bahamas, Sierra Leone,
Liberia, Ivory Coast, Ghana, Nigeria,
South Africa, Namibia, Cuba, Haiti,
Dominican Republic, Jamaica, Virgin Is.,
Windward Islands, Suriname-Guyana,
London, Holland, Burundi, Congo Brazzaville,
Dem. Rep. of Congo,Rwanda, Zambia, Botswana,
Lesotho, Mozambique, Swaziland, Malawi, Zimbabwe*

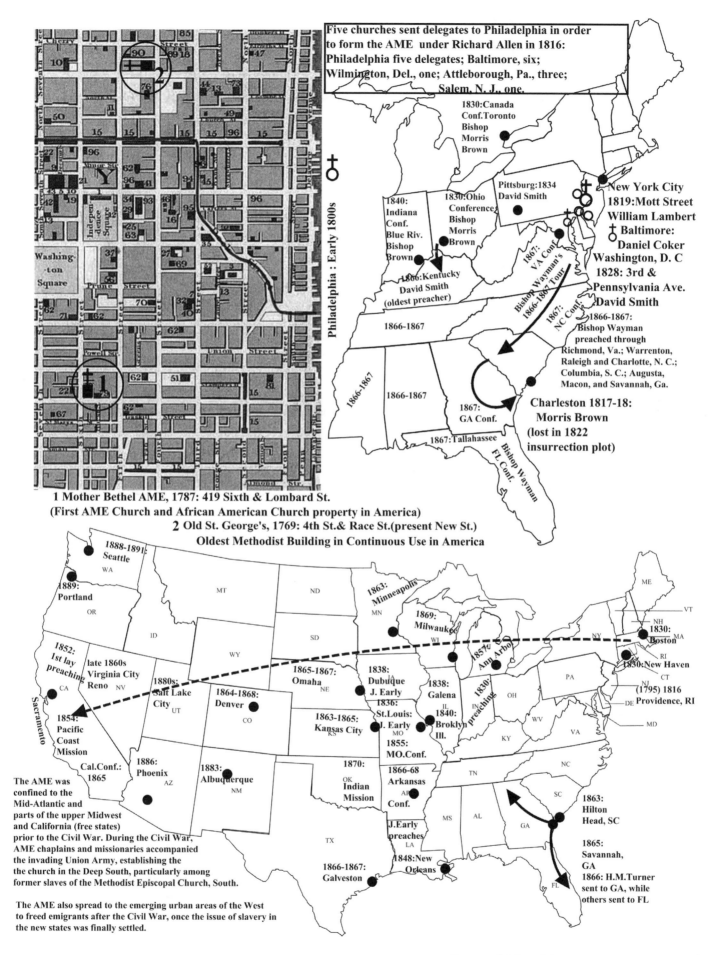

Marching with Zion

Formation and Spread of the African Methodist Episcopal Church Zion

In a similar protest over discrimination in worship, Peter Williams and James Varick led a group to withdraw from John Street Methodist Church in New York City (1796), even as "the Allenites" left St. George's in Philadelphia. While initially receiving pastoral leadership from white Methodist and Episcopal preachers in their own house of worship (built 1800), Williams, Varick, Christopher Rush, Abraham Thompson, and others feared that the Methodist Conference could confiscate their church property due to the provisions in the Model Deed. Highly restricted in their ability to perform pastoral duties, Williams and Varick led the African American church to sever ties with Methodism and legally incorporated their church in March 1801. Although interest was keen, Varick's group declined to affiliate with Allen's churches, and efforts were made to create autonomous churches in connection with the Zion Mother Church. Stronger organization emerged in 1820–1821, and the AME Zion Church was formed with six churches (the name *Zion* was added formally in 1848). In June 1822 at a conference in Philadelphia, three Methodist elders ordained Varick, Abraham Thompson, and Leven Smith; subsequently, James Varick was elected the first term bishop of the new church.

As with the AME, the AME Zion was confined to the free states of the northeast—centered upon New York—until slavery in the Confederate states was dismantled by the Civil War and the Emancipation Proclamation. Even before the Civil War ended, the AME Zion made great gains in the South among the disenchanted freedmen of the Methodist Episcopal Church, South. Entire black congregations of the MECS often voted to transfer into the AME Zion. James Walker Hood (later bishop) became the great AME Zion apostle to the South, building a center for the church from 1864 in New Bern, Wilmington, Fayetteville, and Charlotte, North Carolina. Bishop Joseph Jackson Clinton sent many other preachers marching into the Zion of the "New South" during Reconstruction, enabling him to organize conferences in Louisiana, Virginia, South Carolina, and Alabama, where the AME Zion remains strong today. An interesting feature of the AME Zion is that they struck "male" from their *Discipline* in 1876 and ordained women from 1884. Notable members included Harriet Tubman, Sojourner Truth, and Frederick Douglass.

From 1876, the AME Zion branched out to the African Diaspora, beginning in Liberia. The march continued into Ghana (West Gold Coast 1909, East Gold Coast 1910) and Nigeria (1928). The missionary impulse of the AME Zion continued throughout the twentieth century with new congregations and mergers: Jamaica (1966, merger with United Holy Church); London-Birmingham, England (1971); Mozambique and Malawi (1994); and South Africa (1994-1998). The AME Zion Church today also has solid congregations in Angola, Ivory Coast, Ghana, Guyana, India, St. Croix-Virgin Islands, Trinidad, Tobago, Togo, Zimbabwe, and Swaziland. The denomination operates Livingstone College in Salisbury, North Carolina, and two junior colleges. A merger with the Christian Methodist Episcopal Church has been close to fruition. Yet the AME Zion will not merge without the term "African" in the new church's name. The African Methodist Episcopal Church Zion name testifies to its history—and destiny—as an important part of the worldwide Wesleyan and African church families.

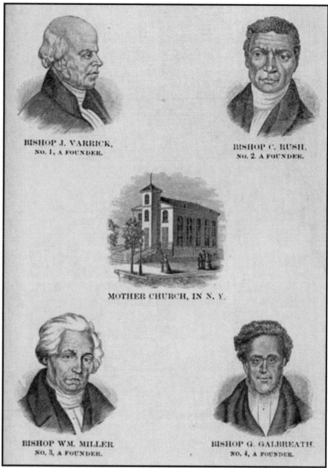

BISHOP J. VARRICK, NO. 1, A FOUNDER.

BISHOP C. RUSH, NO. 2, A FOUNDER.

MOTHER CHURCH, IN N. Y.

BISHOP WM. MILLER, NO. 3, A FOUNDER.

BISHOP G. GALBREATH, NO. 4, A FOUNDER.

Churches and Membership at Organizing Conference, 1820: Zion Church, New York, 763; Asbury Church, New York, 150; Long Island Church, 155; Wesley Church, Philadelphia, 330; East Penn'a., 18; New Haven, 24; total, 1,426

	1821	1831	1864	1880
No. of churches	6	7	131	
No. of bishops	0	2	4	7
No. of conferences	1	2	7	20
No. of ministers	22	39	378	2,500
No. of members	1,426	1,689	13,340	c. 275,000

Latest Statistics and World Distribution: 2005

No. of churches	3,260
Inclusive members	1,440,405
No. of preachers	3,507

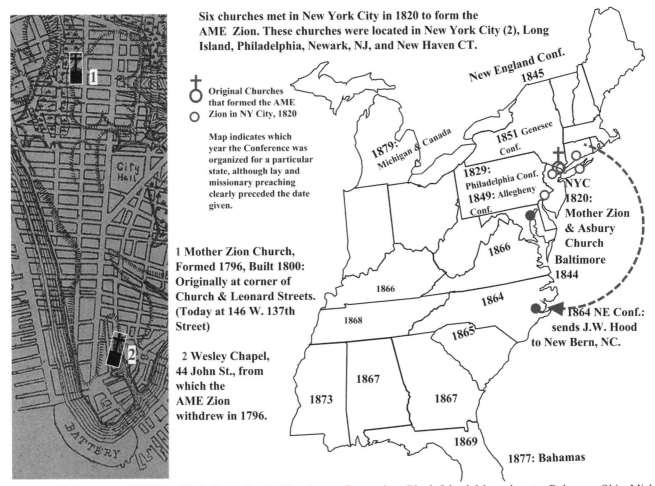

Six churches met in New York City in 1820 to form the AME Zion. These churches were located in New York City (2), Long Island, Philadelphia, Newark, NJ, and New Haven CT.

⚥ Original Churches that formed the AME Zion in NY City, 1820

Map indicates which year the Conference was organized for a particular state, although lay and missionary preaching clearly preceded the date given.

1 Mother Zion Church, Formed 1796, Built 1800: Originally at corner of Church & Leonard Streets. (Today at 146 W. 137th Street)

2 Wesley Chapel, 44 John St., from which the AME Zion withdrew in 1796.

New England Conf. 1845

1879: Michigan & Canada

1851 Genesee Conf.

1829: Philadelphia Conf.
1849: Allegheny Conf.

NYC 1820: Mother Zion & Asbury Church

Baltimore 1844

1866

1866

1868

1864

1865

1864 NE Conf.: sends J.W. Hood to New Bern, NC.

1867

1873

1867

1869

1877: Bahamas

Geographical extent in 1880: New York, Pennsylvania, New Jersey, Connecticut, Rhode Island, Massachusetts, Delaware, Ohio, Michigan, Wisconsin, Illinois, Indiana, Missouri, Kentucky, Tennessee, Alabama, Louisiana, Mississippi, Florida, Maryland, District of Columbia, Virginia, North Carolina, South Carolina, Georgia, Texas, California, and Oregon; in other countries, as Canada, Bahama Islands, Liberia.

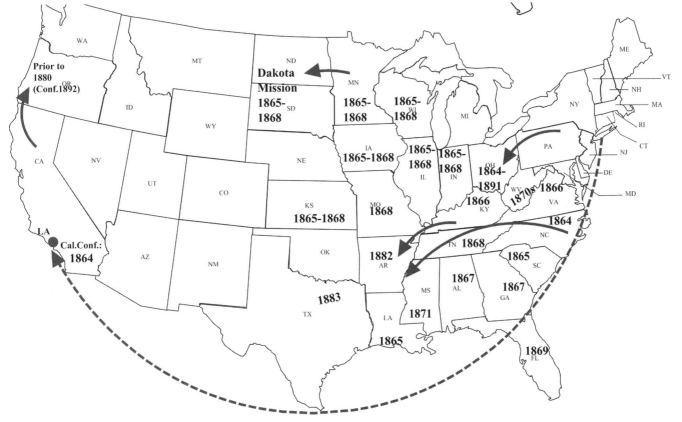

Prior to 1880 (Conf. 1892)

Dakota Mission 1865-1868

1865-1868

1865-1868

1865-1868

1865-1868

1865-1868

1864-1891

1866

1870s

1866

1868

1864

Cal. Conf.: 1864

1882

1868

1865

1883

1871

1867

1867

1865

1869

Methodists Vote for Democracy with Their Feet

The Formation of the Methodist Protestant Church

From the time of the O'Kelly schism of 1792, almost every MEC General Conference debated the question of how democracy should be interpreted in Methodist structures. A significant wing of the church argued for more lay rights in governing the church and for preachers to check the absolute appointive authority of bishops with rights of appeal. In the 1820s, Methodist laity were achieving rising wealth along with the nation, and Jacksonian populism spread the gospel of democratic local self-determinism. Thus dissatisfaction with the episcopal decision-making process prompted the more democratic pastors and congregations to ally themselves in a loose confederation of union societies. From the late 1820s, these union societies began to advocate in the official Methodist press (and later in their own nonofficial journals) for the "mutual assured rights" of laity and itinerant clergy in the face of a dominant episcopacy. In the 1828 General Conference, conservative MEC leaders demanded that the union societies renounce their rebellion against strong episcopal connectionalism. They refused to do so, and it was not long until the union societies sought more organization to put their egalitarian principles into practice. Twelve new annual conferences were formed over the next two years, the first being the North Carolina Conference, formed in Halifax County. Meeting in Baltimore in November 1830, the "Associated Methodist Churches" met to formally organize the conferences into the Methodist Protestant Church.

A number of compromises were necessary for the associated churches to become an independent church. Originally, many of the associated churches were so displeased with the connectional itinerancy that they proposed to do away with it altogether. Though local churches gained more autonomy, the constitution of 1830 did not go nearly as far as congregationalism. Instead, it dispensed with bishops but kept a connectional system with a president of each conference making appointments "subject to revision by a Committee of Appeals." In practice, this evolved into appointments made by the committee in consultation with the president of the conference, and then approved by the conference. The president remained in the pastorate while fulfilling his duties, and the conferences had no office of presiding elder. All elders were equal in rank and could find redress for appointments under appeal. The high ideals of antislavery were too divisive to entertain for the powerful southern conferences such as Maryland, Virginia, and North Carolina. The MPC split in 1858 over the matter but reunified after the Civil War in 1877. Nevertheless, the MPC held segregated conferences in the South into the 1930s. While the union societies had allowed women the right to vote in church matters, no such provision was included in the new constitution. The "mutual rights" of equal lay and clergy representation in annual and General Conference were ratified. Yet local preachers who had enjoyed conference vote in the union societies were denied this right within the new church. At the formation of the MPC, over five thousand of the most democratically inclined members of the Methodist Episcopal Church broke with the mother church. With the passage of time, the MPC and the Methodist Episcopal churches grew closer together in polity. The presidents of the conferences gathered episcopal-like power, and the two Methodist Episcopal churches adopted lay representation in conferences in the late nineteenth and early twentieth centuries. The way was cleared for reunion, which occurred when the MPC joined with the MEC and MEC, South, in 1939 to form The Methodist Church. The Methodist Protestant Church nevertheless stood as a testimony to the strong democratic impulse that evolved and endured in American Methodism.

" 'Tis true she is going down, but like the beautiful Ohio River, the further it goes downstream, the deeper and broader it becomes."
—Asa Shinn, responding to a quip that the MPC "is going down."

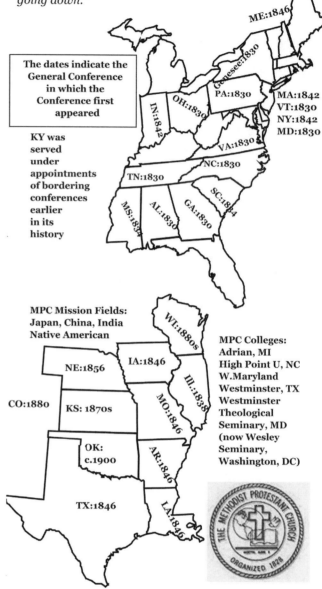

The dates indicate the General Conference in which the Conference first appeared

KY was served under appointments of bordering conferences earlier in its history

MPC Mission Fields: Japan, China, India Native American

MPC Colleges: Adrian, MI High Point U, NC W.Maryland Westminster, TX Westminster Theological Seminary, MD (now Wesley Seminary, Washington, DC)

In 1846, the MPC consisted of 761 preachers, for 59,905 members.

Year	Clergy	Churches	Members
1925	1,082	2,275	189,583
1929	2,175	2,218	195,460
1935	1,095	2,135	199,498

The MPC brought 191,863 members into the reunified Methodist Church in 1939

In through the Out Door

The Wesleyan Methodist Connection Break

From its beginnings in 1784, the MEC had always been strong south of the Mason-Dixon Line. Indeed, 90 percent of its membership had been southern, primarily in Maryland and Virginia, according to the statistics of the Christmas Conference. In the early nineteenth century, national tensions started to simmer as northern states began emancipating slaves and resisting in Congress any new states becoming slave and weakening the abolition movement. In contrast, southern states concerned with maintaining their way of life based on representational power in the face of the free North, began to complain, as John C. Calhoun did, of "the tyranny of the majority." Such regional tensions and arguments began to be transferred to the MEC. As Methodism spread southward into slave states, its membership found it expedient to capitulate to state laws allowing slavery to gather power. Yet once General Conferences became delegated in 1808, the power of southern membership began to wane. Indeed, in the 1812 General Conference, northern delegates first outnumbered southern delegates 38 to 25 (with the Western Conference's thirteen delegates consisting of members on both sides of the Ohio River). Every General Conference afterward, up to 1844 (118 North, 68 South) increased the gap between northern and southern Methodist delegates. This prompted each conference delegation to choose among a polarizing continuum of positions on slavery: from extreme, to mild abolition in the north, to northern centrists who tended to side with the anti-abolition southern moderates simply wanting no more slavery in new states, to a few extreme pro-slavery southern delegations. The voting of the centrists with the southern delegations was designed to keep the MEC from splitting. Effectively, General Conference majorities were built on a set of parliamentary alliances that traded upon exchanging the unity of the church for the injustice of continued slaveholding in the South, under cover of the rhetoric "kindness and mercy to slaves." This did not placate northern abolitionists for long. In the 1836 and 1840 General Conferences, moderates again voted with the southern states to continue to allow Methodists in the South to hold slaves—particularly since so many southern pastors actually held slaves. This was too much for the abolitionists, who saw their desire to end slavery in Methodism as impossible as long as moderates sided with the South. So much energy had been placed in keeping the peace with southern delegates (what Norwood called the "front door to schism") that it was quite a surprise when a group of abolitionist Methodists met in Utica, New York, to create an independent Methodist church ("through the back door," or "exit" to schism). In 1842, Orange Scott and LaRoy Sunderland, ardent abolitionist delegates from the Genesee Conference, led in the formation of a group that seceded from the MEC. In Andover and Utica the following year, they formed the Wesleyan Methodist Connection (adopting "Church" in its name only in 1947). Arguing that their connection represented Wesley's true polity principles, the Wesleyans adopted strong antislavery and anti-episcopacy positions. The first General Conference was held at Cleveland, Ohio, in 1844, where six conferences were constituted, reporting 15,600 members. This new Wesleyan body would have a profound effect on the resolution of the MEC position on slavery at the upcoming 1844 General Conference.

As the Wesleyans grew, they took on a more fervent theological commitment to the Wesleyan notion of entire sanctification. This would lead the new church in the late nineteenth and early twentieth centuries toward affiliation with other holiness groups—both within Methodism and beyond—committed to the doctrine that instantaneous sanctification could be experienced with justification as a distinct "second work of grace." Making their headquarters in Indianapolis, the Wesleyans sought to spread knowledge and vital piety. To that end, they founded several liberal arts colleges including: Houghton College, New York; Central College in South Carolina; and Indiana Wesleyan University. Wesleyans found common cause in spreading vital piety when they joined with the Pilgrim Holiness Church (another Methodist holiness splinter church) in June 1968, forming The Wesleyan Church. In 1994, membership worldwide stood at 223,662, while North American membership was 122,116.

Rev. Orange Scott
(1800-1847)
Founder of The
Wesleyan Methodist Connection
May 1843

Breaking Up Is Not So Hard to Do

The Schism of the MEC and Formation of the Methodist Episcopal Church, South

The Wesleyan schism of 1842 set in motion a rapid swing in the power balance of the MEC at the 1844 General Conference. Meeting on May 1, at Green Street Church, New York City, this one-month-long General Conference would test the principles and polity of the entire church, with profound effects.

Fearing that mild abolitionists would hemorrhage away to join the Wesleyan Methodist Connection, moderates in the North voted with abolitionists to check the power of the southerners. Moderates did so knowing that only through an alliance between themselves and abolitionist delegates would northern conferences have the votes and power in the future to control General Conferences in the aftermath of the Wesleyan schism. To solidify the new veto power the unified northern delegates had over the South, a test case was presented to censure the power of bishops (and pastors) who held slaves. The case grew out of the contention of the northern abolitionists that the General Conference had the power to depose anyone from the episcopacy—particularly in the case of holding slaves contrary to the northern conferences' polity and practice. Bishop James Osgood Andrew of Oxford, Georgia, had married a woman who inherited some slaves from her first husband. At the time, General Conferences elected bishops and required them to be itinerate superintendents, that is, to preside over conferences anywhere in the country. The northern bishops and the General Conference delegates were pushed to resist Andrew's episcopacy, because he would naturally be required to oversee northern conferences. This was a recipe to inflame and further divide the MEC, particularly as the New England Conference and others would split if a slaveholding bishop held power of appointment over pastors in any free states. Thus, the power of the General Conference to regulate the episcopacy in a way to prevent further schism was at stake. Therefore, a series of resolutions was passed calling for Andrew to make one of several choices: either sell the slaves, manumit them, send them to Liberia, or desist from the exercise of his office. However, in Georgia, where Bishop Andrew resided, the law prohibited the manumission of slaves. He feared selling them to others in the South, who might treat them cruelly. The slaves themselves refused to emigrate to Liberia. So the bishop was caught on the horns of quite a dilemma.

A resolution was introduced in the conference that "the Rev. James Osgood Andrew is hereby affectionately requested to resign his office as one of the Bishops of the Methodist Episcopal Church." After several days' discussion, a less harsh substitute for this motion was offered by two members of the Ohio Conference, to the effect "that it is the sense of this general conference that he desist from the exercise of his office so long as the impediment exists." Andrew offered to resign, but his episcopal colleagues from the South urged him to refuse, lest the General Conference receive unquestioned power to remove a bishop for any position contrary to views of the dominant North. On May 31, a motion was made to postpone any further action in the matter until the next General Conference. The South unanimously concurred, and the motion enjoyed mild support from certain members of the middle and northern conferences, hoping once again to avoid schism through a southern alliance. However, it was defeated by a narrow vote of ninety-five to eighty-four. The Ohio substitute

Interior of Green Street MEC, New York City Site of the Andrew Trial and where the Plan of Separation Emerged May 1844

Bishop James O. Andrew (1794–1871) 1st bishop of the MECS

Rev. Joshua Soule (1781–1867) primary author of the MEC constitution (1808), bishop 1824), and original bishop of the Methodist Episcopal Church, South (1846)

Site of the Formation of the MEC, South May 1845, Louisville, KY

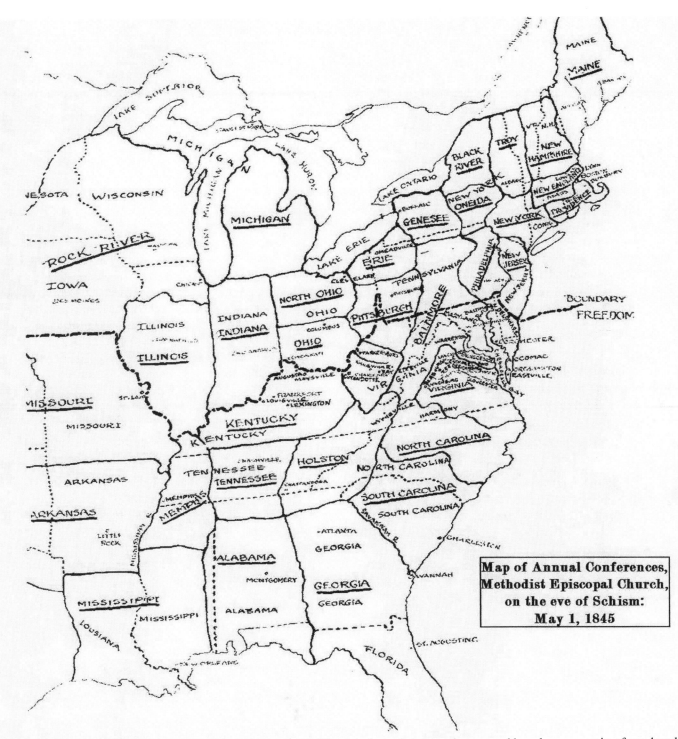

Map of Annual Conferences,
Methodist Episcopal Church,
on the eve of Schism:
May 1, 1845

measure, deposing Bishop Andrew from the episcopacy until he was free of slavery, then passed by a larger margin of one hundred eleven to sixty-nine.

The Andrew test case of 1844 had succeeded: the General Conference was again under abolitionist control. The case had brought the power of the southern episcopacy to account to the general Church, rather than to its own regional cultural and ecclesial practices. However, this dealt a blow to any desire of the southern bishops to submit to a northern-dominated General Conference. They realized correctly that their southern episcopal identity would forever be caught between their southern parish constituencies and the northern conference's power constraints.

Those bishops most in sympathy with southern concerns and the constitutionality of episcopal power being unchecked were Bishops Andrew, Soule, and Morris. They gathered together with other southern delegates in a special session to draw up a detailed plan of separation from the MEC. The plan was adopted on June 8, 1844. By this plan all the property within the limits of the southern organization when formed was to be free from any claim by the General Conference or expansion by any northern conference. The southern church was also to receive an equitable share of the common church property, and so on. Churches in border conferences would be permitted to vote their allegiance to either church. While delegates returning home to both North and South met with disappointed constituencies, and there was a year to prevent the breach, the die was cast.

A southern constituting conference was held at the Fourth Street Church in Louisville, Kentucky, on May 1, 1845. On May 15, the Methodist Episcopal Church, South, was duly organized. In 1848, the General Conference of the northern section of the MEC repudiated the plan of separation, forcing the Church South to sue in federal courts to maintain their rights to property and proceeds of the Publishing House under the plan. Suits were brought in the United States circuit courts in New York and Cincinnati. In the New York suit, a decision was reached in favor of the Church South; but in Cincinnati the case first was adverse to the South. The Cincinnati decision was appealed to the Supreme Court of the United States, where on April 24, 1854, Justice John McLean overturned the earlier decision, and the plan of separation was sustained in all its provisions. If the divorce settlement was clear, the notion of where the "kids" would live was an open and volatile matter. A number of border conferences and churches were split about whether to affiliate with the MEC or the MECS: the Baltimore, Virginia, and Missouri Conferences, along with churches along the Ohio River in Kentucky and Ohio, as well as the eastern shore of Virginia. While the divorce was settled, the new parties had to learn to live their own new lives. The MECS elected new bishops: Andrew and Joshua Soule affiliated South (Thomas Asbury Morris going North), and new bishops were elected: William Capers, Hubbard Hinde Kavanaugh, George Foster Pierce, and others. While the old doctrinal standards remained unchanged, polity developed understandably so that the episcopacy was more powerful than the southern General Conference. Once the Supreme Court decision was reached in 1854, a publishing house was set up in Nashville, which became the headquarters for the MECS (Atlanta and Louisville were narrowly outvoted).

Thus by 1845, the church of Wesley that preached the unity of conferencing as a means of encountering the grace of God was now divided into three main groups (MEC, MECS, MPC), and four smaller ones (Republican Methodists, AME, AMEZ, and Wesleyans). Though by no means alone as a trans-regional church that split over slavery and its constitutional entanglements (Presbyterians 1837, Baptists 1845), the schism of the powerful Methodist Church foreshadowed the secession of the Southern States and the national tragedy of the Civil War. As U.S. Grant, himself an infrequent Methodist, claimed, "There were three parties in American politics, Republican, Democrat, and Methodist." Now that unifying power was itself a house divided. Indeed, as Henry Clay observed, the cords of the country were snapped with the split of the Methodist Church.

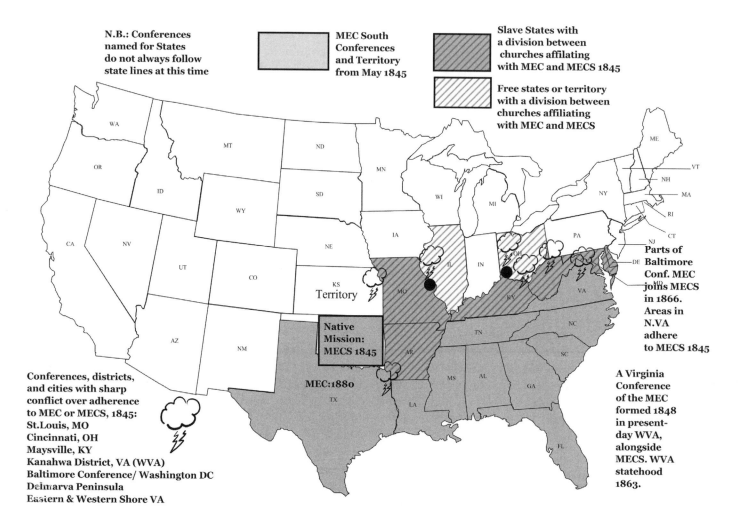

The Blues and the Abstract Truth

Slave Missions and the Uneasy Conscience of Southern Methodism

In 1826, 40 percent of Carolina and Georgia Methodists were slaves. Most historians regard southern Methodism's mission to slaves as, at best, a weak attempt to ameliorate the most pernicious effects of slavery, and, at worst, guilty overcompensation. Yet from 1787 to 1829 integration was the primary goal of American Methodism, with much of its center of gravity in the South. Methodism's Arminian theological commitment to Christ's atonement for the entire world (and not the elect) meant something in that southern time and place. Such theology was not co-opted totally by southern plantation politics and economics. It committed southern Methodism—as no other institution in the South—to the ministry and education of slaves bound to those behind "that peculiar institution." Yet, quite literally, southern Methodism "owned" the burden of ministry to slaves.

John Wesley's own experience in ministry to slaves on South Carolina plantations had provoked him to observe that colonial American slavery was pure evil. Nevertheless in only a few years after the formation of the MEC, the spirit, and more often even the law of the *Discipline* became adapted to civil and state laws concerning slavery. Methodism found it expedient for its extension southward to soften its stance on slaveholding among Methodists—even Asbury paled to the British Thomas Coke's antislavery principles.

Even before the formation of the MECS, southern Methodist leaders under the leadership of South Carolinian William Capers had taken up Wesley's crusade in South Carolina of almost a century earlier: to minister to and educate slaves. The same resistance was encountered by Wesley and Capers—the fear on the part of plantation owners that Methodism would humanize their property. Capers, as superintendent of missions (and himself a slaveholder) responded to a powerful politician's request to send two missionaries to the Ashley and Santee River area plantations in 1829. Capers was a complicated yet competent missionary. One of his first assignments was to slaves in Wilmington, North Carolina, and then he sent out African American preachers (against the civil and ecclesiastical law) from Charleston, South Carolina, into the interior. From 1840, Capers' mission leadership and able publication of the *Southern Christian Advocate*, inspired similar mission work to slaves in most of the southern conferences from Georgia to South Carolina (Charleston), to Kentucky, to Texas. He developed a catechism with a dual purpose: for children and slaves, "A Catechism for Little Children and for Use on the Missions to the Slaves." By the split in 1844–1845, this catechism was the standard for instructing the slaves across southern Methodism—continuing until the emancipation of all slaves in America in 1863 and the final surrender of the Confederacy at Appomattox, Virginia, in 1865.

The formation and development of the MECS within its battle for legitimacy against the northern branch surely contributed to the narrative of southern Methodist eagerness to minister to slaves, proving southerners were "true heirs and representatives of Wesley's movement." Yet clearly the work of the MECS created a critical mass of awakened and learned African American Methodists with an enduring, unintended consequence: the southern Methodist missions provided education and ministry among African American slaves. After the Civil War, this work would flower into a critical mass that freed southern Methodists would capitalize on to found the independent Colored Methodist Episcopal Church (CME, 1870).

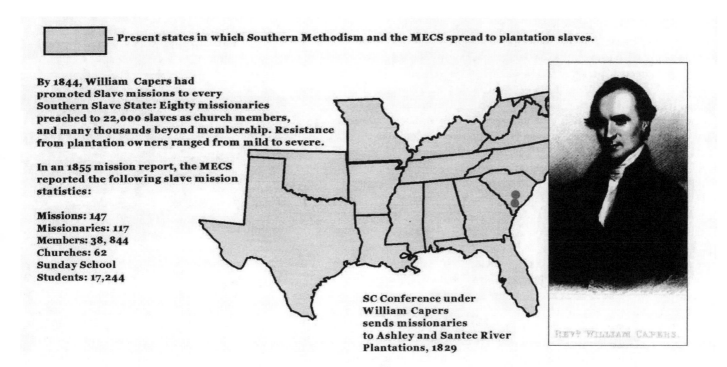

= Present states in which Southern Methodism and the MECS spread to plantation slaves.

By 1844, William Capers had promoted Slave missions to every Southern Slave State: Eighty missionaries preached to 22,000 slaves as church members, and many thousands beyond membership. Resistance from plantation owners ranged from mild to severe.

In an 1855 mission report, the MECS reported the following slave mission statistics:

Missions: 147
Missionaries: 117
Members: 38, 844
Churches: 62
Sunday School Students: 17,244

SC Conference under William Capers sends missionaries to Ashley and Santee River Plantations, 1829

REV⁴ WILLIAM CAPERS.

Brave Hearts

Methodists Encounter Native Americans

Native Americans were the closest neighbors to circuit riders in practically all the new territories that American Methodism ventured into in the nineteenth century. Yet the encounter was slow: Native American independence, the vast interior, and the Methodist preacher's need to secure hospitality from settlers, rendered interactions with natives as tenuous. The first successful Methodist work among natives of North America began as late as 1801 in the Credit River territory of Canada.

As Methodism moved into Ohio in the early 1800s, the density and penetration of Methodist circuit riders forced natives and circuit riders to interact. The first sustained Methodist work among native peoples was with the Wyandottes in northern Ohio. The traction of the mission came from an unlikely source: the mission was established by a free-born African American and native mulatto, John Stewart. Poverty-stricken and struggling with alcohol, Stewart had been converted (while half inebriated) at a camp meeting in 1814. He soon sobered up and preached his story of conversion among diverse audiences. Through a hired interpreter, he began preaching to the Wyandottes, resulting in the conversion of his interpreter and several chiefs. He baptized, performed marriages, and administered the sacraments, even though he was not approved for licensing as a preacher until 1818. On August 7, 1819, the Ohio Annual Conference established the first official Methodist mission to Native Americans and assigned James Montgomery, a local preacher, as its first missionary. The first itinerant appointment was James B. Finley, the "Old War Horse" who led the mission from 1823 to 1827. Here lie the ironic beginnings of Methodist mission to Native Americans and, indeed, the world.

The agent who stimulated preaching beyond district- and conference-approved boundaries—lay preacher Stewart—provoked an institutional response to protect Methodist episcopal power in the region. The extra-conference success of Stewart's preaching with the Wyandotts quickly drew the attention of MEC bishops. They created the Methodist Missionary Society in 1819 to raise funds and appoint regular Methodist preachers beyond the usual circuit boundaries. The lay nature of Methodism, its Wesleyan Arminian theology that deemed Christ's death as efficacious for the entire world, and its circuit riders' presence on the extreme frontiers, combined to create a question for the movement: Can the Methodist mission go forward beyond the boundaries of conferences in the hands of self-appointed laity like Stewart? Or must there be an agency under episcopal oversight that selects and directs Methodist mission among Native Americans, and indeed the widest horizons of the earth? Wesleyan connectional theology, combined with a host of new encounters with non-Christians beyond self-supporting circuits, created a need for a new mission society where bishops could select and send pastors for the necessary fields. In 1819, the Methodist Missionary Society was constituted. From 1819 until 1833, the society solicited funds and sent preachers only among the Native Americans in North America.

The centers of Methodist mission to natives were co-extensive with some of the proudest of Native Americans: from the Wyandotte of Ohio, to the Creek and Cherokee in Georgia and North Carolina, Methodist ministers were working effectively even before Andrew Jackson's removal act of 1830 promoted the "trail of tears." Many of the great Eastern tribes were forced to government lands but found Methodists quickly arriving to at least slightly ameliorate the suffering of relocation: Shawnee to Kansas, Choctaw, Creek, Cherokee, Chickasaw, and Seminole to the eastern Oklahoma Territory— Methodist missionaries sought to witness to these uprooted natives as early as any other westward sojourners. Later in 1842 the peaceful Wyandottes of Upper Sandusky, Ohio, were forced to relocate to Oklahoma as well. All of these tears were the seeds that marked a trail for Methodist ministry beyond the Mississippi Valley.

**John Stewart Preaching to
the Wyandotte in Ohio, 1814**

**James B. Finley, First Itinerant
Methodist Preacher among
the Wyandotte in Ohio, 1823**

Principal Chief of the Creek Nation, Samuel Checote and his family in front of their home in Okmulgee

SAMUEL CHECOTE
Grave 1.9 miles N.W.

This noted Creek leader, born 1819 Ala., had attended old Asbury Mission before he came to Ind. Ter. He was a Methodist preacher for 32 years till his death, 1884. He served as Lieut. Col., First Regt. Creek Mounted Vols., C.S.A., during the Civil War. Elected for his first term as Principal Chief, Creek Nation, in 1867.

Today, most Native American Methodist work is located in the Oklahoma Indian Mission Conference--comprised of 89 United Methodist churches in Oklahoma, Kansas and Texas. As of 2006, approximately 8,300 members are in OIMC; 33 churches are in the Southeast region, serving primarily Choctaw and Chickasaw tribal members; 12 churches are Apache, Caddo, Comanche, Delaware, Kiowa, and Wichita congregations. In the Northeast region, 33 churches serve Cherokee, Creek, Seminole and Yuchi, congregations.The Central region is composed of several urban congregations and includes the tribal peoples of Ponca, Pawnee, and Cheyenne/Arapaho. About 98 percent of OIMC clergy and lay missioners are Native Americans, representing approximately 15 people groups. The first annual conference session of the then "Indian Mission" was held in 1844 at Riley's Chapel at Park Hill, Oklahoma. Several Choctaw congregations have been around for over 150 years.The first Kiowa Methodist congregation, over 100 years. The churches of the OIMC are the original parent conference of Oklahoma.

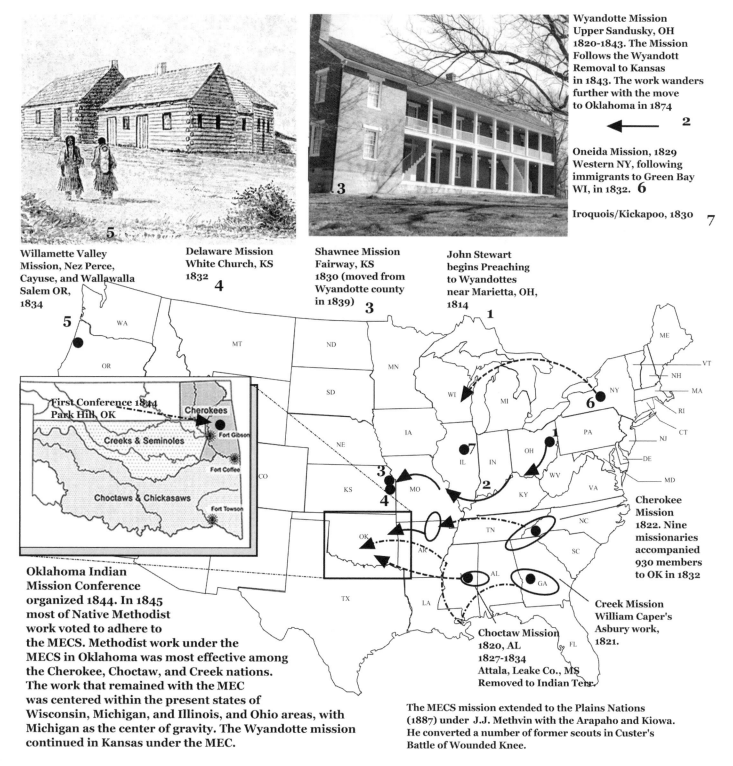

Wyandotte Mission Upper Sandusky, OH 1820-1843. The Mission Follows the Wyandott Removal to Kansas in 1843. The work wanders further with the move to Oklahoma in 1874

2

Oneida Mission, 1829 Western NY, following immigrants to Green Bay WI, in 1832. 6

Iroquois/Kickapoo, 1830 7

Willamette Valley Mission, Nez Perce, Cayuse, and Wallawalla Salem OR, 1834
5

Delaware Mission White Church, KS 1832
4

Shawnee Mission Fairway, KS 1830 (moved from Wyandotte county in 1839)
3

John Stewart begins Preaching to Wyandottes near Marietta, OH, 1814
1

First Conference 1844 Park Hill, OK

Cherokees
Fort Gibson
Creeks & Seminoles
Fort Coffee
Choctaws & Chickasaws
Fort Towson

Oklahoma Indian Mission Conference organized 1844. In 1845 most of Native Methodist work voted to adhere to the MECS. Methodist work under the MECS in Oklahoma was most effective among the Cherokee, Choctaw, and Creek nations. The work that remained with the MEC was centered within the present states of Wisconsin, Michigan, and Illinois, and Ohio areas, with Michigan as the center of gravity. The Wyandotte mission continued in Kansas under the MEC.

Cherokee Mission 1822. Nine missionaries accompanied 930 members to OK in 1832

Creek Mission William Caper's Asbury work, 1821.

Choctaw Mission 1820, AL 1827-1834 Attala, Leake Co., MS Removed to Indian Terr.

The MECS mission extended to the Plains Nations (1887) under J.J. Methvin with the Arapaho and Kiowa. He converted a number of former scouts in Custer's Battle of Wounded Knee.

Good, Bad, and Ugly

The MEC Becomes Adjunct to the United States Army in the Civil War

Once the War Department issued the order in May 1861 for regimental chaplains, the MEC was one of the largest providers of chaplains to the Federal Armies. Ironically, only after the Emancipation Proclamation (January 1, 1863) did the General Conference enact legislation barring slaveholders from membership. The total number of Methodist chaplains who served in the Union armies during the war can be safely put at well over 500. In 1861, the MEC had fifty conferences, with 2,759 preachers, not including its mission areas overseas, the work on the Pacific Coast, and some US territories in the interior. The vast bulk of MEC pastors who enlisted as chaplains in the US Army came from the New England and mid-Atlantic states—the states that had already achieved emancipation well before the war. A considerable number of pastors, however, came from the border states. Even a few MECS pastors in the border states enlisted as chaplains in the Federal Army. In addition to preaching regularly to their regiments, chaplains were also the distributing agents for the American Bible Society, the Tract Society, and the various aid and sanitary commissions—such as the US Christian Commission. Faithful work was done in caring for the sick, for prisoners, and in providing reading as a more helpful distraction to various forms of soldierly dissipation. Millions of Bibles, tracts, books, and sermons spread the Christian vision of a godly America across the battle camps. Millions of dollars in aid was raised. Yet the good that chaplains did could not fully ameliorate the ugliness of war. Ironically, mixed in with the sea of American and Methodist blood, the country was awash with Christian literature. On the Union side, the MEC provided over 300,000 troops (almost a third of the standing US Army). The war caused 600,000 casualties, ten times the number of casualties as in Vietnam. It clearly reduced a generation of American youth, and disproportionately among the young men of the MEC and the MECS.

According to William Warren Sweet's *The Methodist Episcopal Church and the Civil War* (Cincinnati: Methodist Book Concern, 1912), the number of chaplains and the MEC conferences they hailed from are listed as follows: Baltimore 2; Iowa 17; Black River 8; Kansas 11; Central German 1; Kentucky 4; Central Illinois 13; Maine 4; Central Ohio 13; Michigan 8; Cincinnati 21; Minnesota 10; Des Moines 2; Missouri and Arkansas 13; Detroit 12; Nebraska 1; East Baltimore 17; Newark 12; East Genesee (NY) 6; New England 10; East Maine 9; New Hampshire 10; Erie 10; New Jersey 11; Genesee 10; New York 8; Holston 1; New York East 2; Illinois 21; North Indiana 13; Indiana 21; North Ohio 12; Northwest Indiana 11; Southern Illinois 17; Northwest Wisconsin 4; Troy 10; Ohio 17; Upper Iowa 2; Oneida 6; Vermont 7; Philadelphia 21; West Iowa 2; Pittsburgh 18; West Wisconsin 5; Providence 5; West Virginia 13; Rock River 13; Wisconsin 5; Southeast Indiana 9; Wyoming 6; for a total of 487 (Sweet indicates that perhaps another 20 or so pastors served as chaplains without being listed through their conference, such as bishops. He puts the total number safely at 510).

The MEC provided twice the number of chaplains to the US Army (500+) than the MECS provided to the Confederate Army (240+). This would be roughly proportional with the membership (2:1) and the number of itinerant preachers in each church (2,500+: 1,500+) , except for the fact that so many more MECS pastors enlisted and fought as officers (another 140+).

The bishops of the MEC at the time—especially Matthew Simpson (1), Edmund Janes (2), and Edward Ames (3)—offered the direct services of themselves and their preachers to important Civil War causes: Simpson became friend and counselor of President Lincoln, who traveled widely and used his magnificent oratory to elicit support for Lincoln and emancipation—even preaching the president's eulogy; Edmund Janes led Methodist work in the US Christian Commission—an aid and public service charity that cared for thousands of wounded and needy soldiers; and Edward Ames, who was a chaplain in an Indiana regiment, led the absorption of southern Methodist churches under orders of Secretary of War, Edwin M. Stanton. Until President Lincoln clarified the order that only churches without pastors be occupied, Ames's mission work in the South was done with the support of the War Department. The MEC effectively became a division in the Army under the command of Bishop Ames. Obviously this aggravated relations with the MECS and closed options for reconciliation after the war. Indeed, after the war, there were ten MEC conferences in the South (with churches in major cities like Atlanta, New Orleans). The MEC actually emerged from the war relatively unscathed and, certainly in terms of territory and membership, somewhat strengthened. More importantly, the MEC enjoyed an almost national-church status, with Matthew Simpson becoming chaplain to a president and a nation. He leveraged his national platform to become a pastor and fund-raiser among a growing, wealthy, urban, northern industrialist elite. After the war, Simpson's flock would bankroll the course of Methodism westward and to the world.

Matthew Simpson

1

Edmund Janes

2

Edward Ames

3

Southern Exposures

The Spread and Survival of the Methodist Episcopal Church, South

At the formation of the MECS in 1845, there were sixteen conferences spread across the states that allowed slavery. Three new conferences were added at the General Conference in Petersburg, Virginia, in 1846: the St. Louis, Louisville, and Louisiana Conferences, in states where there was a clear division of loyalties. According to *A History of the Methodist Episcopal Church, South, in the U.S.* by Alexander Gross (New York: The Christian Literature Company, 1894), at the first General Conference the following statistics were reported: 459,659 members, 1,519 traveling preachers, 2,833 local preachers, with 124,961 colored members (p. 49). Almost immediately, the MECS launched into mission across a wide front. During the time between 1846 and the 1850 General Conference at St. Louis, missions to slaves (1846) and Native Americans in Oklahoma (1846) already formed were continued and strengthened by the MECS. A Chinese mission in Shanghai (1848) was constituted. Work in California had begun in 1850 as Southerners rushed to find gold in "them thar hills," and bishops sent preachers behind them to find spiritual gold in those Forty-niners. Conferences spread and were constituted in Arkansas and the Kansas territory mission (1854). In order to support these initiatives with Christian knowledge, the MECS took its winning division of property from the 1854 Supreme Court case and created a Southern Methodist Publishing House in Nashville. From this time onward, Nashville became the de facto MECS headquarters and continues today to house The United Methodist Publishing House, as well as many other General Agencies serving The United Methodist Church nationally and internationally. One interesting piece of Methodist polity was being omitted from the *Discipline* in those very printing offices. From 1858 at the Nashville General Conference, the prohibition against slavery was stricken from the General Rules in the *Discipline*. The conference cited adherence to the Article of Religion, which mandated support of the laws of the US government, to prevent church agitation against slavery in the states where the laws of the government allowed slavery. Such church policy allowed the MECS to quickly consolidate its base among slave-owning and sympathetic parishioners—as seen in these statistics in 1858: Traveling preachers: 2,577; local preachers: 4,984; Caucasian: 499,694; African American: 188,036; Native American: 3,874; Total membership MECS: 699,165. This represents a total gain of over 1,000 itinerant preachers, and almost a quarter of a million adherents after only fourteen years.

At the start of the Civil War, the MECS consisted of 757,205 total members, with roughly two-thirds Caucasian and one-third of its population slaves (with a small but growing Native American mission in Oklahoma and Kansas). All the successes in numbers, however, could not mask southern Methodism's captivity to regional, cultural, economic, and political patterns dependent upon slavery. Yet American Methodism as a whole went to war motivated by the goals of local flags, rather than a national or global Wesleyanism committed to the cross and the flame. Ironically, crosses and flames were perhaps never more apparent in Methodist history than during the Civil War, 1861–1865. Numbers do not tell the full story of pain and loss. But statistics demonstrate the heartbreaking reality of how both Northern and Southern heirs of Wesley went to war with each other—as chaplains and, in many cases, officers. William Warren Sweet's doctoral thesis from the University of Pennsylvania presents the raw data on which conferences fielded chaplains and soldiers. The data depict a southern church on the march, with more Methodist pastors serving as officers in the Confederacy than their northern counterparts in the Union Army. Chaplaincy was the largest form of active duty in either army. This list of Confederate chaplains from the Methodist Episcopal Church, South, totals at least 242. No Minutes were returned for the Missouri, St. Louis, Kansas Mission, or the Pacific Conferences during the four years of the war. At least twelve chaplains from the MEC, South, in West Virginia, Kentucky, and Missouri served the Union Army. Besides these regular chaplains, a considerable number of ministers performed visitation and ministry duties with the

This list of Confederate chaplains from the Methodist Episcopal Church, South totals at least 242. No Minutes were returned for the Missouri, St. Louis, Kansas Mission, or the Pacific Conferences during the four years of the war.

At least 12 chaplains from the MEC, South in West Virginia, Kentucky, and Missouri served the Union Army.
Besides these regular chaplains, a considerable number of ministers performed visitation and ministry duties with the Confederate Army, similar to the ministerial delegates of the United States Christian Commission.

A remarkably large number of MECS ministers were commissioned as combatant officers and in the ranks. Total: 141

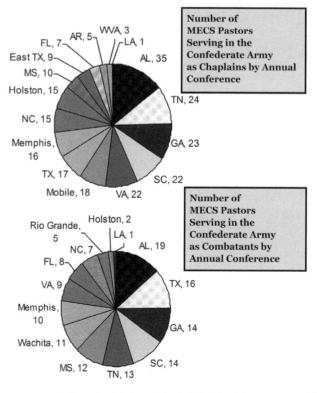

Number of MECS Pastors Serving in the Confederate Army as Chaplains by Annual Conference

WVA, 3; LA, 1; AL, 35; FL, 7; AR, 5; East TX, 9; MS, 10; Holston, 15; NC, 15; Memphis, 16; TX, 17; Mobile, 18; VA, 22; SC, 22; GA, 23; TN, 24

Number of MECS Pastors Serving in the Confederate Army as Combatants by Annual Conference

Rio Grande, 5; Holston, 2; LA, 1; AL, 19; NC, 7; FL, 8; VA, 9; Memphis, 10; Wachita, 11; MS, 12; TN, 13; SC, 14; GA, 14; TX, 16

Confederate Army, similar to the ministerial delegates of the United States Christian Commission. A remarkably large number of MECS ministers were commissioned as combatant officers and in the ranks—total: 141.

The Federal Army struck at the heart of the MECS when it occupied Nashville in February 1862, capturing the crown jewel of southern Methodism—its publishing house. Adding insult to injury, the printing presses were turned from printing sheets of biblical learning to broadsheets for the Federal Government Printing Office. Equipment not useful for government purposes was damaged and destroyed, and it would be years before the debts of southern Methodist publishing could be liquidated and new initiatives launched. Good ministry was done in Confederate camps, though oftentimes sermons focused more on avoiding evils such as drinking and gambling than on the more nuanced Wesleyan distinctives. Tracts and Bibles were given out in conjunction with the American Bible Society. Notable revivals led by Confederate Methodists broke out early in the war among Lee's Army of Northern Virginia—especially in religious Stonewall Jackson's Corps. Later as the war ground on, foxhole religion seemed to lose some of its luster, though numerous Arkansas regiments in the Western theater from 1863 to 1864 experienced revival. Nevertheless the war was hard on southern Methodist pastors and parishioners, with quite a difference between the florid early war religio-political rhetoric and the sobering realities of 1864–1865. The MECS was decimated, along with the Southern economy and ethos: the MECS total membership dropped by a third—from 750,000 to less than 500,000 at the end of the war. Festering feelings over the MEC occupation of southern Methodist churches in conjunction with Federal armies closed off any cooperative possibilities for reconciliation after the close of hostilities. Meeting at Palmyra, Missouri, in June 1865, southern delegates reluctantly accepted God's judgment on the (secular) South, but committed the MECS to renewed independence in light of perceived MEC breaches of the Plan of Separation.

For the MECS, the way through Reconstruction would, however, be an uphill one. Little oversight of the annual conferences could be exercised during the war, and even the 1862 General Conference in New Orleans was impossible to mount—only weakening the connectional bonds that were tearing apart all over the country. An important set of decisions would face the MECS at the 1866 General Conference in New Orleans: what blessed ties could bind the MECS, as well as bind its physical wounds? Answers came: the strong and historic Baltimore Conference adhered to the MECS in 1866, bringing confident leadership less sullied by secession and the war; consultation with freed black leaders approved their desire for independence; the class meeting was relegated from obligatory to voluntary; and the six-month probation for membership abolished in efforts to make membership more attractive in the post-war South. Most notably, lay representation in general and annual conferences was adopted, releasing new leadership and resources. These decisions created an energy and a direction for southern Methodists to expand remarkably through Reconstruction—nationally and internationally: Japan 1872, Mexico 1873, Brazil 1876, Korea 1889, Cuba 1899, Poland and Czechoslovakia in post-World War I Europe 1920.

Reconstruction actually served the MECS. An institution not under government control, the Methodist Episcopal Church, South, gave southern Wesleyans a welcomed outlet for self-determination. The long road to reunion would be challenging, requiring a number of initiatives: a readjustment toward the African American Southern Methodists (with the creation of the CME Church in Jackson, Tennessee, in 1870 to set up the wishes of freedmen for self-determination); the Cape May Commission's regular formal meetings and informal fraternal efforts at Methodist reunion starting in the 1870s; and a forward progressivism shaped by Bishop Atticus Haygood's influential vision of a "New South" and "Our Brother in Black" of the 1880s. If not progressive, the MECS patiently learned to practice a vision beyond provincialism: through its enduring goal of mission, its chastened political instincts, its inspiring pastoral rhetoric, its confident episcopal leadership, and its early unleashing of lay leadership.

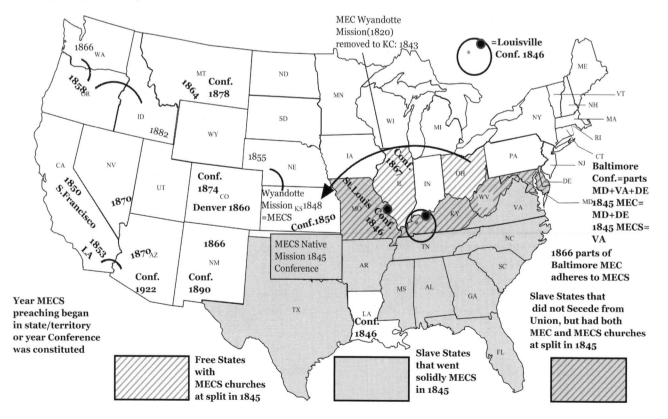

Free, Free, Set Them Free

The MEC Freedman's Aid Society, and the Rise of the CME from the MECS

The Freedman's Aid and Southern Education Society of the Methodist Episcopal Church was founded in August 1866. It evolved out of the Western Freedman's Aid Commission in Cincinnati, soon after the Emancipation Proclamation of 1863. Its intention was to provide secondary and higher education to the freed slaves during Reconstruction, as well as to supply education for all the poor in the South after the Civil War. By 1900, the society supported over forty-seven colleges, reporting almost an even distribution between black and white colleges. The society's report for 1897 indicated over three thousand students under instruction. From the inception of the society to the turn of the twentieth century, the MEC through the society had educated over one hundred thousand students. Many of the well-known historically black colleges in the United States have grown from the Freedman's Aid work of the MEC. On the next page is a map from 1921 showing the distribution of these colleges, giving the year of their founding.

Beyond its own "reconstruction," the MECS put its efforts into helping its freed black members establish the Colored (later Christian) Methodist Episcopal Church. Already losing more than 207,766 black members during the war, particularly to the AME and AMEZ southern missions, southern Methodists of all races appreciated their neighbor's desire to maintain independence. Under the initiative of black leaders in consultation with the MECS, a petition was proposed in 1866 for self-determination. The MECS agreed to the petition, and a plan was developed to turn over church properties and provide ordinations and episcopal consecrations for the new church. At the MECS General Conference in 1870 at Memphis, Tennessee, the plan was ratified. Bishops Robert Paine and Holland N. McTyeire (who later helped found Vanderbilt University), provided both ecclesial and financial assistance to the new church, which formed in Jackson, Tennessee, on December 15, 1870. The first bishop consecrated was William Henry Miles, who went on to serve for twenty-two years. Another bishop was consecrated in 1870, Richard Vanderhorst. In 1873, in Augusta, Georgia, three more bishops were elected, who served well into the first third of the twentieth century: Joseph A. Beebe, Lucius Holsey, and Isaac Lane. These leaders sought to avoid using the pulpit for political redress, and they stressed education for the new CME, founding Lane Institute/College in 1882; Paine College (after the MECS bishop) 1882; Miles College; Texas College; and Philips School of Theology. The Church vigorously pursued evangelization and went from 75,000 members and fifteen annual conferences in 1874, to today when the CME reports over 800,000 members, thirty-four annual conferences, and three thousand churches worldwide, including Africa, Haiti, and Jamaica.

Holland N. McTyeire
(1824-1889)

William Henry Miles
(1828-1892)

Joseph A. Beebe
(1832-1903)

Lucius H. Holsey
(1842-1920)

Isaac Lane
(1834-1937)

MEC Colleges Founded in the South by the Freedman's Aid Society: From 1866
= year established by Freedman's Aid Society

Tennessee Wesleyan, formerly U.S. Grant College, was founded in 1857, supported by The Freedman's Aid Society.
It was located in Athens, TN, to educate the poor in Holston Conference. Central Tennessee College (1866) became Fisk University,
founded by Clinton B. Fisk of the TN Freedman's Aid Society. New Orleans College (1869) became Dillard University. In 1925, the
George R. Smith College of Sedalia, Mo. (where Scott Joplin studied music in 1896) burned. In 1933, it merged with Philander Smith
College. Morgan College was founded as Centenary Biblical Institute by the Baltimore Conference Freedman's Aid Society in 1867. It
became Morgan College (1890), now Morgan State University.

Original Conferences of the CME
and subsequent expansion before 1900

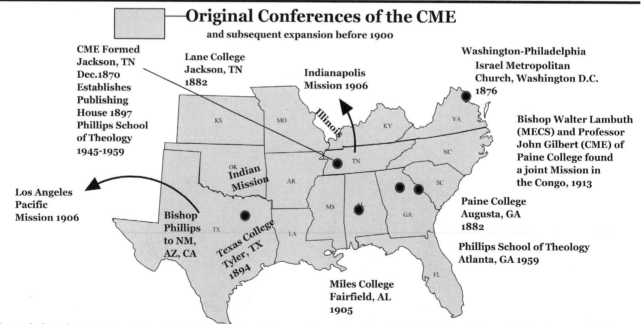

Episcopal plan of 1873, Bishop Miles held the Missouri and Kansas, Tennessee, North Mississippi, and Kentucky Conferences; Bishop
Beebe, the Virginia, North Carolina, South Carolina, and Georgia Conferences; Bishop Holsey, the Florida, Arkansas, Mississippi, and
Alabama Conferences; and Bishop Lane, the Northwest Texas, East Texas, and Louisiana Conferences. Each bishop itinerated across
these Conferences from 1873 until shortly prior to their deaths.

1920 statistics: 267,366 members, 3,402 traveling preachers, 3,285 churches, and ten educational institutions.

Free to Move about the Country

MEC Church Extension in City and Country, 1860–1900

Even before the Civil War ended, northern Methodism was on the march. Once mobilized, the chaplains and workers for the various aid organizations sought expanded horizons of ministry. With their newfound experience beyond the local and regional church, and supported by the money of the wealthy industrialists of the North, the MEC spread benevolence in many ways south and west. In May 1864, the Church Extension Society was created as the fourth general agency of the church, two years after the Homestead Act spurred western migration. Its task was to raise, donate, and lend money for the construction of new churches, particularly in the West, where congregations were few and often financially limited. The Board of Church Extension, as it was called from 1873, effectively raised millions of dollars, distributing it to support the final geographic push of the MEC into the mountain and desert states of the western interior. Leaders such as C. C. McCabe were able to raise funds and inspire preachers to go West through his nationally known story of heroic service as a Civil War chaplain and prisoner of war in Libby Prison. Under McCabe's pithy slogan, "We're building two a day," the Church Extension Society raised 6.9 million dollars, and built 11,677 churches by the end of the century. Soon his example sparked the MECS to form its own Church Extension Society. The MEC closed out the last half of the nineteenth century by growing from around 750,000 members in 1850, to almost 3 million in 1900.

Other avenues to aid developed from North to South. With the Emancipation Proclamation, the slaves of the South were suddenly free, but often without education or skills to effectively maintain self-sufficiency. To address this need, northern philanthropists became highly interested in providing education and training through Freedmen's Aid societies. The MEC, with money and pastors experienced as chaplains in the South during the war, founded its Freedman's Aid Society in August 1866 at Cincinnati. It was instrumental in founding such educational institutions as Clark University, Central Tennessee College, and Claflin University. Many historically black colleges were products of northern (and southern) Methodism after the Civil War. Nevertheless, these positive initiatives were often perceived in the Reconstruction South as more Northern aggression to dominate the already depleted South. But by the 1880s, a more progressive wing of southern Methodists gathered around the inspirational racial vision of a New South, espoused eloquently by Bishop Atticus Haygood. Not all in the North believed it: Frederick Douglass queried, "Has anyone seen this New South?" Mistrust continued between the North and South in both secular and sacred matters. Yet both churches were about to encounter wider issues.

Immigration to the US in the late nineteenth and early twentieth centuries (24 million from 1880 to 1920) was unprecedented. Both churches quickly called attention to the needs of the new immigrants in the cities and where they spread out across the plains and into the West. Having often neglected its own northeastern urban base, the MEC needed to evolve new forms of urban ministry. Enter Lucy Rider, who formed the deaconess movement in Chicago, focusing on the needs of poverty-stricken urban women and children. The movement began in 1888 and quickly spread to other cities. In 1902, the MECS formed its own deaconess board—founded by Belle Bennett—for the growing southern cities. The Women's Home Missionary Societies of both churches started numerous urban ministries as well. Immigration and the grinding poverty of new industrialization called for a just response. Through the deaconess ministry coupled with strategic outreaches of the WHMS into the gateway immigration cities, Methodism responded. Here also was stimulus for the great home mission of the MEC and MECS to Germans, Swedes, Norwegians, Danes, Italians, and others. By 1900, both the MEC and the MECS had organized language conferences for these new arrivals. Coupled with the Pacific home mission to Asians (and effective Native American work), Methodism on the North American continent was preaching and worshiping in many tongues. That Methodism could become so at home among those seeking a new home was a foretaste of the translatable character of the Wesleyan message. Indeed, lessons learned in home mission would provide a vision for foreign mission. Ironically, these responses may still have much to teach us as we search for ways to engage America's new international populations.

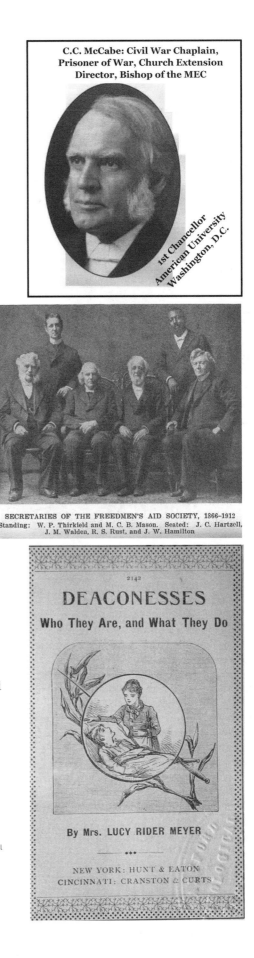

C.C. McCabe: Civil War Chaplain, Prisoner of War, Church Extension Director, Bishop of the MEC

1st Chancellor American University Washington, D.C.

SECRETARIES OF THE FREEDMEN'S AID SOCIETY, 1866–1912
Standing: W. P. Thirkield and M. C. B. Mason. Seated: J. C. Hartzell, J. M. Walden, R. S. Rust, and J. W. Hamilton

2142

DEACONESSES
Who They Are, and What They Do

By Mrs. LUCY RIDER MEYER

NEW YORK: HUNT & EATON
CINCINNATI: CRANSTON & CURTS

Deaconess Blues: Deaconess Work and Women's Home Mission Society Ministry Among the Lost and the Least, ca. 1900

The duties of the M.E. Deaconess are described in the consecration service:

"You are to minister to the poor, visit the sick, pray with the dying, care for the orphan, seek the wandering, comfort the sorrowing, save the sinning, and relinquishing wholly all other pursuits, devote yourselves to such forms of Christian labor as may be suited to your abilities."

The deaconess office was created within the Church of the United Brethren in Christ (1897).
The Evangelical Association (1903), and the Methodist Protestant Church (1908) later followed.

● = MEC Deaconess Homes, Under the Authority of The Women's Home Mission Society from 1885 to 1900

Chicago National Training Center for Domestic, Home, and Foreign Mission Founded by Lucy Rider Myer 1885 Recognized by General Conference, 1888

New England Deaconess Home and Training Center, 1889

Deaconess Home Brooklyn & Training Center, NY

Aldrich Home Grand Rpds.

Cunningham Orphanage Urbana

Detroit Home

Buffalo Home

Cleveland Home

Pittsburgh & Phil. Home

Jersey City & Ocean Grove Deaconess Homes

Wilmington Home

Deaconess Home Baltimore

D.C. Deaconess Home & Sibley Hospital

Logan

Salt Lake City & Provo Homes

Deaconess Home Denver

Des Moines

Scarritt Kansas City

Louisville

Nashville

Knoxville

S.Fran. Deaconess Home

LA Deaconess Home

(Map state abbreviations: MT, ND, MN, SD, WY, WI, MI, NY, ME, VT, NH, MA, RI, CT, NJ, DE, MD, IA, NE, IL, IN, OH, WV, VA, CA, NV, UT, CO, KS, MO, KY, TN, NC, SC, AZ, NM, OK, AR, MS, AL, GA, TX, LA, FL)

Methodist Deaconess Work (Locally Incorporated and Supported by Annual Conference):

Agard Deaconess Sanitarium, Lake Bluff, IL
Asbury Hospital and Rebecca Deaconess Home, Minneapolis, MN
Bethany Hospital, Kansas City, KS
Bloomington Deaconess Hospital, IL
Deaconess Institute, Amsterdam, NY
De Peyster Hospital, Verbank, NY
Elizabeth Gamble Deaconess Home and Hospital, Cincinnati, OH
Elizabeth Haas Deaconess Home, St. Paul, MN
Fall River Mass. Deaconess Home
Freeport Ill. Deaconess Home
German Deaconess House, Cincinnati, OH
Bear Deaconess Home and Hospital, Spokane, WA
Deaconess Home and Hospital, Omaha, NE
Deaconess Home, Milwaukee, WI
Montana Deaconess Home and Hospital, Great Falls, MT
New England Deaconess Home, Boston, MA
New York Deaconess Home, NYC
Providence Deaconess Home, RI
Rockford Deaconess Home, IL
Terre Haute Deaconess Home, IN

(by the 1920s both the MEC and MECS Deaconess Locations had multiplied beyond ability to map at this scale)

● = MECS Deaconess Work (from 1902) under the Women's Home Mission Society (founded in 1890)

1892 Scarritt Bible and Training School, headed by Maria Gibson, is opened in Kansas City, MO, thanks to the efforts of Belle Harris Bennett (M.E. Church, South). In 1902 Scarritt began training deaconesses.

1924, the Kansas City school is moved to Nashville, TN, where it became Scarritt College for Christian Workers.

1897 Sue Bennett Memorial School in London, Kentucky, was built by the Woman's Board of Home Missions of the M.E. Church, South.

In April 1903, the Woman's Missionary Society of the Louisville Conference, Methodist Episcopal Church, South, founded the Louisville Settlement Home.

"Here Extensions": MEC Church Extension West and Home Mission—Civil War to 1900

1866 =MEC Extensions, by year into States and Conferences coextensive with the MECS 1845-1900

Alaska: 1904

Hawaii: Pacific Japanese, 1900
Hawaii Conference, 1905

MEC Home Mission Language Conferences (All Integrated by 1938)
East German=EG 1864
German=G 1845
Chicago German= CG 1872
N.W. German=NWG 1864
S.W. German=SWG 1864
West German=WG 1879
Southern German=SG 1874
St.Louis German=STLG 1879
Pacific German=PG 1905

Italian = I 1909
Eastern Swedish=ES 1901
Northern Swedish=NS 1894
Central Swedish=CS 1894
Western Swedish=WS
N.W. Swedish=NWS 1877
S. Swedish= SS 1912
N.W. Norwegian=NWN 1880
Norwegian-Danish=ND 1885
W.Norw.-Danish=WND 1892
Central German=CEG 1864

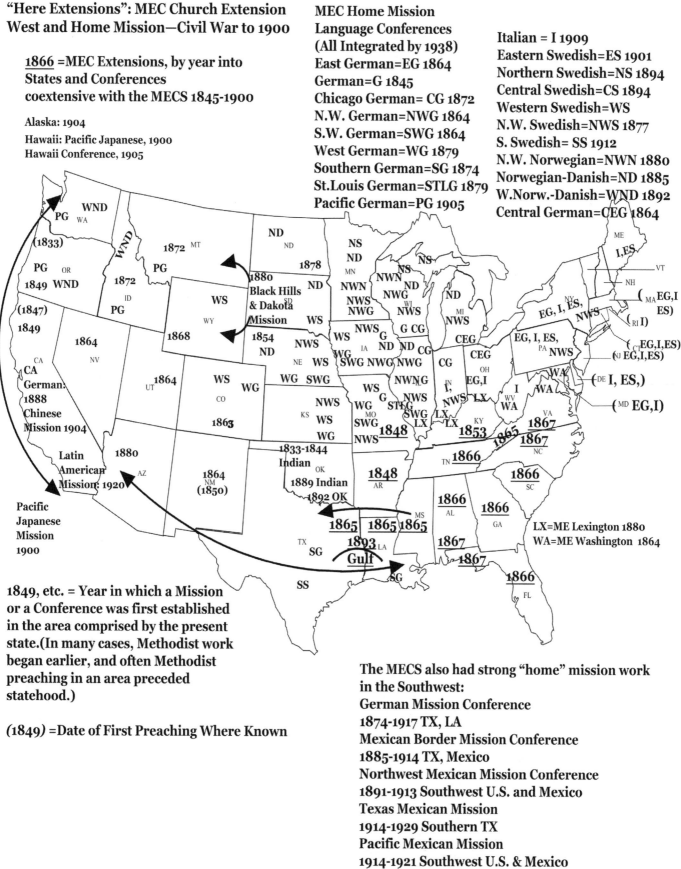

1849, etc. = Year in which a Mission or a Conference was first established in the area comprised by the present state.(In many cases, Methodist work began earlier, and often Methodist preaching in an area preceded statehood.)

(1849) =Date of First Preaching Where Known

The MECS also had strong "home" mission work in the Southwest:
German Mission Conference
1874-1917 TX, LA
Mexican Border Mission Conference
1885-1914 TX, Mexico
Northwest Mexican Mission Conference
1891-1913 Southwest U.S. and Mexico
Texas Mexican Mission
1914-1929 Southern TX
Pacific Mexican Mission
1914-1921 Southwest U.S. & Mexico
Western Mexican Mission/Conference
1918-1939 Western states beyond Pecos River

Going On to Perfection with a Head Start

The Free Methodists and Holiness Movements

Already before the Civil War, Methodists in both the North and the South were concerned about the fast pace of change in American society. As the largest church in America, Methodism—as a connectional church—ironically became the civil religion of the country at the same time the country was dividing. Methodism from the late 1830s to the early 1840s experienced a number of divides, along lines of class, race, region, and theology that only deepened in the late nineteenth century. Methodism in the North had not kept pace with the immigrant growth in the cities in the industrial age. In the South, both before and after the Civil War, Methodism existed in class and race segregations that exposed the Wesleyan ideals of personal and social holiness as hollow. Some of these currents were clearer among MEC women in the northern cities. In 1836, Sarah Worrall Lankford started the Tuesday Meeting for the Promotion of Holiness in New York City. Her sister, Phoebe Palmer (1), experienced what she called "entire sanctification" in 1837 and began leading the Tuesday Meeting. Women found this group and others like it a way to express leadership denied to them in official church structures. In 1859, Palmer published *The Promise of the Father,* in which she argued in favor of women in ministry. Indeed, many of the arguments for going back (and on) to Wesleyan entire sanctification were advanced by Palmer.

Apart from these days of small beginnings, Methodism had risen in class well beyond its core principles. The Five Points Mission and the Palmers, through their national preaching and publishing, were effective in putting the question of entire sanctification again before the entire Wesleyan connection.

Yet some, particularly a group of pastors in the Genesee Conference in western New York, called for a more radical retrieval of Methodism's historic connection between spirituality and social justice. Long considered the "Burned over District," the Genesee Conference was regionally receptive to emotional revival. From within this context, leaders such as Benjamin Titus Roberts (2) arose to call the MEC to account. In the areas of injustice to slaves and the wealth of the powerful classes in Methodism, Roberts and others called for a response—a return to holiness as the personal and public expression of the Wesleyan distinctive of sanctification. Even before the Civil War, holiness groups began to gather in revivals, camp meetings, and city missions—such as Phoebe Palmer's Five Points Mission and holiness ministry in New York City. It was clear that some of the renewal efforts could be baptized and absorbed by the Methodist power structures. Indeed, no less a friend to the powerful and wealthy as Bishop Matthew Simpson attended and supported Palmer's mission in New York. Yet the clear Wesleyan commitments to egalitarianism, small group accountability across racial and financial barriers, and the desire to transform society could not be fully realized from the top down. Roberts, and others, particularly objected to the common practice of renting pews, along with membership in secret societies, which Methodism's *nouveau riche* had enthusiastically adopted in the North. Roberts called for the abolition of these signs of respectability as betrayals of true Wesleyanism in addition to his criticism of "New School" Methodist worship and polity. He soon called for a rededication to a more literal reading of Wesley's conversion accompanied by a second work of grace through instantaneous, entire sanctification. Yet Methodist leaders in Buffalo resisted his reforms and attempted to censure Roberts in 1857. Consequently, B. T. Roberts led in the founding of the Free Methodist Church (3) at Pekin, New York, in 1860. The movement attracted followers primarily from Robert's Genesee Conference and the Rock River Conference in Illinois, through the work of John Wesley Redfield. Yet it was a movement that signaled larger theological developments ahead.

As the nineteenth century wound down, the holiness movements within American Methodism took ever greater organizational shape, with the formation of vital holiness associations. These associations developed many regular campgrounds, attracting like-minded believers interested in personal and social transformation. They eventually splintered into many holiness denominations. The largest of these were the Church of God, Anderson, Indiana (4) (1880); Church of the Nazarene (5) (1908); and the Pilgrim Holiness Church (1897). The Pilgrims merged with the Wesleyan Methodists in 1968 to form the Wesleyan Church (6), also headquartered in Anderson, Indiana. (One group held out from the 1968 Wesleyan Church merger, taking the name Bible Methodist Church (7), centered in Ohio and Alabama.) Once independent, many of these holiness groups soon found the organization of their own denomination too confining. By 1910, disaffected Methodists and persons touched by the Holiness Movement were experiencing profound religious awakenings. Former Methodist and holiness leaders were involved in the early Azusa Street Revivals in California. Methodism, through its core values, had once again stimulated a theological renewal beyond its own official structures: national and international Christian renewal through the Pentecostal explosion. Thereby, Wesleyan movements proved still capable, through new forms, to "spread scriptural holiness and reform the nation(s), beginning with the churches."

CHURCH OF GOD
Anderson, Indiana

THE WESLEYAN CHURCH

The Twentieth Century

The twentieth century found Methodists, curiously, coming together and pulling apart in new and often bewildering patterns. With the demise of the solid verities of Protestant America in the late nineteenth century and innate Methodist competitiveness in North America chastened, Methodism reconfigured regional and religious ties. This set in motion a century-long struggle to create new unions, alliances, national agencies, and transnational bodies to reinterpret Methodist identity against the background of the growing power and centralization of the United States government.

In the twentieth century, the West went to war with itself twice. It drew the entire world into old historical conflicts in a profound global engagement that forever changed local connections between church and state. World Wars I and II tested Wesleyan core values and theological commitments, and clearly found them wanting. The Wesleyan worldwide connection was clearly altered in the postwar era: weakened in some areas, but strengthened through self-determination in others. The twentieth century demonstrated that Wesleyans have found it harder to hold together their global connections than it has to put up fences for national, local, tribal, and personal protectionism. In moments of international (and, indeed, national) crisis, Wesleyans have proved as vulnerable as any other Westerners to go to war against each other following their national flags. The tendency to "go local" under stress has been a feature also at the congregational and national levels of Methodism throughout the last century.

The twentieth century has been labeled the American Century, for its rise to international geopolitical prominence. For American Wesleyans in that century, the search for a unified identity nationally, regionally, and indeed through a world connection has proved mixed at best. More often than not, Methodism's instincts for moving globally, then rooting deeply into to soil of every new frontier (wherever that was) often gave rise to serious investments in new settings through institution building. This often had the unintended effect of leaving marginal peoples to organize and promote their own interests through caucuses competing for recognition through national and international boards, and the financial apportionments that support such connectional structures. It is ironic that in this century, Methodists became united as never before, through such international ecumenical work of Methodist layperson John R. Mott, who stimulated the International Mission Council, around which the World Council of Churches organized in 1950. Conversely, Methodism reconsolidated its own family traditions and came together across some of its oldest regional and ethnic identity divides with both the 1939 and 1968 reunions. Often overlooked is how the 1939 union ultimately enshrined the old fears and divides of northern and southern Methodism in a five-regional jurisdictional system, which segregated Methodism's African Americans and their churches into a sixth Central Jurisdiction. Today we live through structures such as the jurisdictions and, above all, the Judicial Council, designed to provide mechanisms that referee the old regional (and racial) divides that are still too much within United Methodism. Ironically, however, new notions of American and Methodist identity emerged in the twentieth century that divided churches even on the local level—in ways that the regional jurisdictions themselves could not contain. Throughout the last third of the twentieth century, Methodism appeared vulnerable not only to the threat of regional splits but also to schism along theological, ethnic, political, and sexual lines.

No sooner had Methodists decided to unite with the EUBs in 1968 than they found our nation divided ever more sharply: on Vietnam, women's rights, race, and gender—all of which could not be reconciled solely with appeal to the Articles of Religion, Wesley's Sermons, the EUB Confessions of Faith—nor even to Scripture itself. So much effort was spent on the polity of United Methodist union that questions of theological difference were delayed. It soon was clear that it would be difficult to define or defend what united us as United Methodists. Choosing the name "United," rather than the close runner-up "Evangelical Methodist Church," only papered over the deep divides of late-twentieth-century Methodism. Such questions prompted the formation of a theological commission to define what united this new United Methodist Church. Led by Perkins School of Theology professor Albert Outler, the commission discerned prophetically and diplomatically that the answer did not lie in the title "United"; that is, what united us was not a commitment to a theological product or creed. Rather, the answer lay in the rich history of the term *Methodist*; that followers of Wesley have been historically committed to a method that takes seriously what Scripture says to us, what our reason says to us, what our tradition says to us, and what our experience in each culture says to us concerning our faith. Thus, at the 1972 General Conference in Atlanta, Outler's Theological Commission gave us what Wesley did not—a "Quadrilateral": committing our church to do theology with a method that honored Wesleyan sources, but allowed the Church to differ on various points under a broad tent. Thus, it is not the "United" aspect of our name that marks our Methodist identity, but perhaps, properly, it will be certain methods that challenge us to be more "United" and "Methodist" in the future. Even in our worship and hymnal tradition, Methodists have found it curiously difficult to decide what we should sing and look like together while in worship. Yet most of the century we have gone on to find ways to sing and worship together in ways that honor our theological and ethnic diversity. When general or annual conferences are about to split over an issue, prudent bishops still call for a break to sing a Charles Wesley hymn!

The Methodist family all over the world will continue to live with the tensions of how to express faith in local terms, while still remaining called to a Wesleyan connection larger than any one local or national church. Such tensions do not translate easily to a tidy historical atlas. As United Methodism celebrates its first forty years, the remainder of this atlas is dedicated to locating where Methodist movements have intersected with important national and international issues. As such, we have marked on maps a number of "altars," representing where we—like Abraham—have wandered and worshiped among new places and faces. Perhaps by connecting these points and paths, we may see patterns to which Wesleyans of every stripe have been curiously blind, yet continue to bind us together deeply across space and time.

The Methodist Experience in America, 1884-1910: Places of Consolidation and Innovation

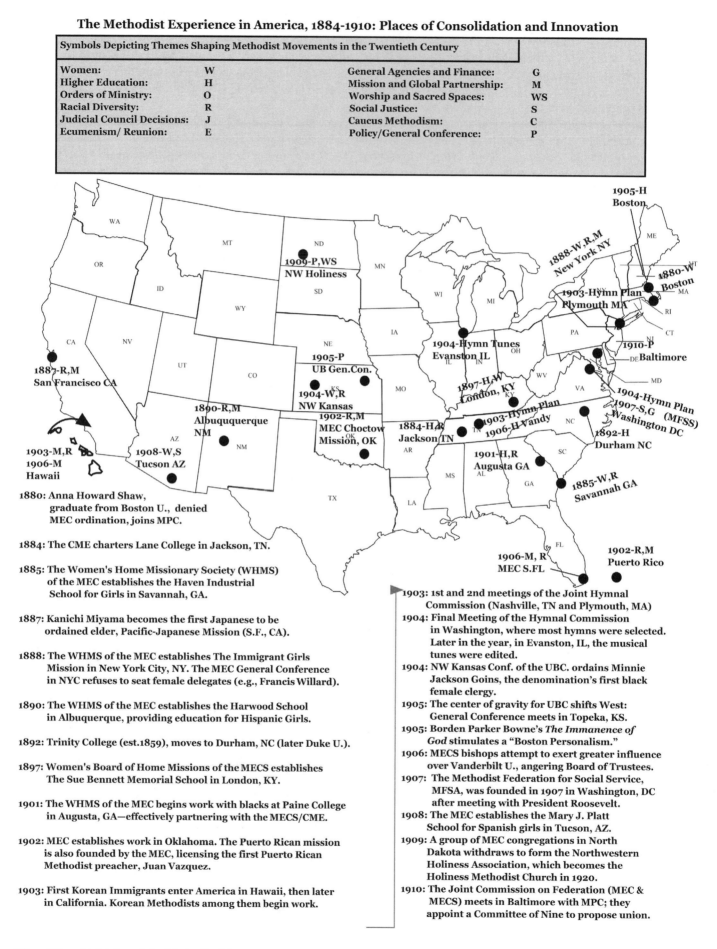

Symbols Depicting Themes Shaping Methodist Movements in the Twentieth Century

Women:	**W**	General Agencies and Finance:	**G**
Higher Education:	**H**	Mission and Global Partnership:	**M**
Orders of Ministry:	**O**	Worship and Sacred Spaces:	**WS**
Racial Diversity:	**R**	Social Justice:	**S**
Judicial Council Decisions:	**J**	Caucus Methodism:	**C**
Ecumenism/ Reunion:	**E**	Policy/General Conference:	**P**

Map labels:
1905-H Boston
1888-W,R,M New York NY
1880-W Boston
1903-Hymn Plan Plymouth MA
1910-P Baltimore
1909-P,WS NW Holiness
1904-Hymn Tunes Evanston IL
1905-P UB Gen.Con.
1904-W,R NW Kansas
1902-R,M MEC Choctow Mission, OK
1884-H Jackson TN
1897-H,W London, KY
1903-Hymn Plan
1906-H Vandy
1904-Hymn Plan
1907-S,G (MFSS) Washington DC
1892-H Durham NC
1901-H,R Augusta GA
1885-W,R Savannah GA
1887-R,M San Francisco CA
1890-R,M Albuququerque NM
1908-W,S Tucson AZ
1903-M,R 1906-M Hawaii
1906-M, R MEC S.FL
1902-R,M Puerto Rico

1880: Anna Howard Shaw, graduate from Boston U., denied MEC ordination, joins MPC.

1884: The CME charters Lane College in Jackson, TN.

1885: The Women's Home Missionary Society (WHMS) of the MEC establishes the Haven Industrial School for Girls in Savannah, GA.

1887: Kanichi Miyama becomes the first Japanese to be ordained elder, Pacific-Japanese Mission (S.F., CA).

1888: The WHMS of the MEC establishes The Immigrant Girls Mission in New York City, NY. The MEC General Conference in NYC refuses to seat female delegates (e.g., Francis Willard).

1890: The WHMS of the MEC establishes the Harwood School in Albuquerque, providing education for Hispanic Girls.

1892: Trinity College (est.1859), moves to Durham, NC (later Duke U.).

1897: Women's Board of Home Missions of the MECS establishes The Sue Bennett Memorial School in London, KY.

1901: The WHMS of the MEC begins work with blacks at Paine College in Augusta, GA—effectively partnering with the MECS/CME.

1902: MEC establishes work in Oklahoma. The Puerto Rican mission is also founded by the MEC, licensing the first Puerto Rican Methodist preacher, Juan Vazquez.

1903: First Korean Immigrants enter America in Hawaii, then later in California. Korean Methodists among them begin work.

1903: 1st and 2nd meetings of the Joint Hymnal Commission (Nashville, TN and Plymouth, MA)

1904: Final Meeting of the Hymnal Commission in Washington, where most hymns were selected. Later in the year, in Evanston, IL, the musical tunes were edited.

1904: NW Kansas Conf. of the UBC. ordains Minnie Jackson Goins, the denomination's first black female clergy.

1905: The center of gravity for UBC shifts West: General Conference meets in Topeka, KS.

1905: Borden Parker Bowne's *The Immanence of God* stimulates a "Boston Personalism."

1906: MECS bishops attempt to exert greater influence over Vanderbilt U., angering Board of Trustees.

1907: The Methodist Federation for Social Service, MFSA, was founded in 1907 in Washington, DC after meeting with President Roosevelt.

1908: The MEC establishes the Mary J. Platt School for Spanish girls in Tucson, AZ.

1909: A group of MEC congregations in North Dakota withdraws to form the Northwestern Holiness Association, which becomes the Holiness Methodist Church in 1920.

1910: The Joint Commission on Federation (MEC & MECS) meets in Baltimore with MPC; they appoint a Committee of Nine to propose union.

1910-1939: Places of Consolidation and Innovation

1913: MECS opens the Lake Junaluska Assembly near Waynesville, NC, as the "Southern Chautauqua."

The MEC forms the first Wesley Foundation at the University of Illinois.

1914: The Tennessee Supreme Court awards control of Vanderbilt University to Trustees and not MECS bishops.

MECS establishes two new seminaries: Emory University in Atlanta (established by Asa Candler, founder of Coca-Cola, and his brother, Bishop Warren Candler) and Southern Methodist University in Dallas.

American University, Washington D.C. admits its first students, with four women.

1918: MECS creates a War Work Commission in D.C. to support U.S. intervention against Germany (WWI).

1919: Centennial of the Methodist Missionary Society raises more pledges than receipts; missionaries recalled. A "Methodist World's Fair" held in Columbus, OH.

1921: MECS relief efforts after WWI form churches in Poland and Czechoslovakia.

The EA establishes Red Bird Mission in KY.

1923: MEC votes overwhelmingly for the Plan of Union with the MECS.

1924: The MEC establishes Gulfside Assembly (African American) in Waveland, MS.

1925: The Plan of Union between the MEC and MECS fails without the three-fourths Conference vote in the South.

1932: The MEC General Conference votes for US membership in the League of Nations.

1935: The MEC, MECS, and MPC publish a second joint hymnal--emphasizing modernism.

1939: The MPC, the MEC and MECS unite as The Methodist Church (MC), Kansas City, KS.

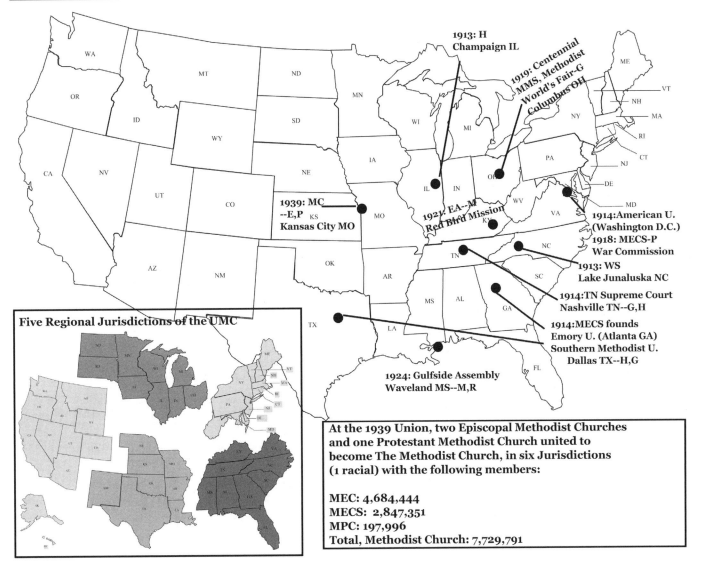

1913: H Champaign IL

1919: Centennial MMS, Methodist World's Fair-G Columbus OH

1939: MC --E,P Kansas City MO

1921: EA--M Red Bird Mission

1914:American U. (Washington D.C.)

1918: MECS-P War Commission

1913: WS Lake Junaluska NC

1914:TN Supreme Court Nashville TN--G,H

1914:MECS founds Emory U. (Atlanta GA) Southern Methodist U. Dallas TX--H,G

1924: Gulfside Assembly Waveland MS--M,R

Five Regional Jurisdictions of the UMC

At the 1939 Union, two Episcopal Methodist Churches and one Protestant Methodist Church united to become The Methodist Church, in six Jurisdictions (1 racial) with the following members:

MEC: 4,684,444
MECS: 2,847,351
MPC: 197,996
Total, Methodist Church: 7,729,791

1940-1956: The Methodist Church—Centralizing in a Globalizing America

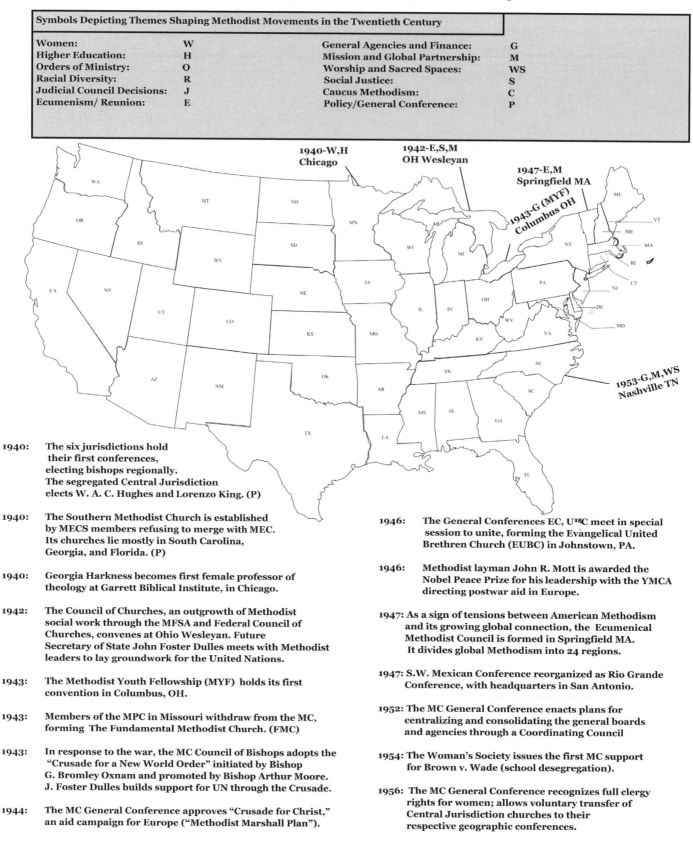

Symbols Depicting Themes Shaping Methodist Movements in the Twentieth Century

Women:	W	General Agencies and Finance:	G
Higher Education:	H	Mission and Global Partnership:	M
Orders of Ministry:	O	Worship and Sacred Spaces:	WS
Racial Diversity:	R	Social Justice:	S
Judicial Council Decisions:	J	Caucus Methodism:	C
Ecumenism/ Reunion:	E	Policy/General Conference:	P

1940-W,H
Chicago

1942-E,S,M
OH Wesleyan

1947-E,M
Springfield MA

1943-G (MYF)
Columbus OH

1953-G,M,WS
Nashville TN

1940: The six jurisdictions hold their first conferences, electing bishops regionally. The segregated Central Jurisdiction elects W. A. C. Hughes and Lorenzo King. (P)

1940: The Southern Methodist Church is established by MECS members refusing to merge with MEC. Its churches lie mostly in South Carolina, Georgia, and Florida. (P)

1940: Georgia Harkness becomes first female professor of theology at Garrett Biblical Institute, in Chicago.

1942: The Council of Churches, an outgrowth of Methodist social work through the MFSA and Federal Council of Churches, convenes at Ohio Wesleyan. Future Secretary of State John Foster Dulles meets with Methodist leaders to lay groundwork for the United Nations.

1943: The Methodist Youth Fellowship (MYF) holds its first convention in Columbus, OH.

1943: Members of the MPC in Missouri withdraw from the MC, forming The Fundamental Methodist Church. (FMC)

1943: In response to the war, the MC Council of Bishops adopts the "Crusade for a New World Order" initiated by Bishop G. Bromley Oxnam and promoted by Bishop Arthur Moore. J. Foster Dulles builds support for UN through the Crusade.

1944: The MC General Conference approves "Crusade for Christ," an aid campaign for Europe ("Methodist Marshall Plan").

1946: The General Conferences EC, UBC meet in special session to unite, forming the Evangelical United Brethren Church (EUBC) in Johnstown, PA.

1946: Methodist layman John R. Mott is awarded the Nobel Peace Prize for his leadership with the YMCA directing postwar aid in Europe.

1947: As a sign of tensions between American Methodism and its growing global connection, the Ecumenical Methodist Council is formed in Springfield MA. It divides global Methodism into 24 regions.

1947: S.W. Mexican Conference reorganized as Rio Grande Conference, with headquarters in San Antonio.

1952: The MC General Conference enacts plans for centralizing and consolidating the general boards and agencies through a Coordinating Council

1954: The Woman's Society issues the first MC support for Brown v. Wade (school desegregation).

1956: The MC General Conference recognizes full clergy rights for women; allows voluntary transfer of Central Jurisdiction churches to their respective geographic conferences.

1956: Maude K. Jensen, former missionary to Korea, is first ordained woman to receive full connection to an annual Conference (Central Pennsylvania).

1957: The Hinton Rural Life Center is established in Hayesville, NC, as a small church retreat center.

1961: Julia Torres Fernandez ordained as the first Hispanic/Latina woman in full connection (Puerto Rico Provisional Conference).

1963: The MC Woman's Division dedicates the Church Center for the United Nations as a resource and lobbying presence to the UN.

1963: Twenty-eight Methodist pastors in the Mississippi Conference condemn racism in the statement "Born of Conviction."

1964: The General Board of Missions is reorganized; the Woman's Society is renamed the Women's Division, and much of their mission is reassigned to the National and World Divisions.

1966: The MC General Conference meets in special session with the EUBC General Conference; they approve the Plan of Union to create The United Methodist Church (sends it to conferences).

1966: The MEC publishes a new version of The Methodist Hymnal (with more traditional Wesleyan selections of tunes, texts and rituals, just as Protestantism undergoes major liturgical renewal).

1967: Good News Movement is formed by Rev. Charles Keysor to promote Methodist evangelical renewal, in Elgin, IL.

1967: The last session of the Central Jurisdiction (MC) meets in Nashville.

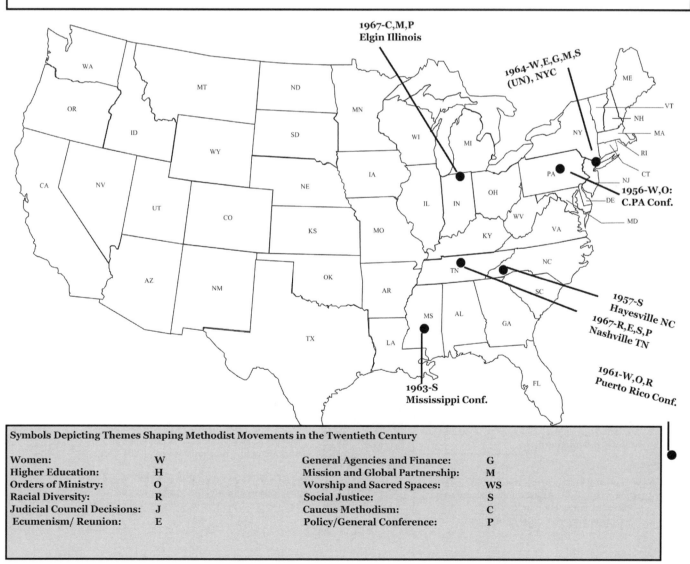

1967-C,M,P
Elgin Illinois

1964-W,E,G,M,S
(UN), NYC

1956-W,O:
C.PA Conf.

1957-S
Hayesville NC
1967-R,E,S,P
Nashville TN

1961-W,O,R
Puerto Rico Conf.

1963-S
Mississippi Conf.

Symbols Depicting Themes Shaping Methodist Movements in the Twentieth Century

Women:	W	General Agencies and Finance:	G
Higher Education:	H	Mission and Global Partnership:	M
Orders of Ministry:	O	Worship and Sacred Spaces:	WS
Racial Diversity:	R	Social Justice:	S
Judicial Council Decisions:	J	Caucus Methodism:	C
Ecumenism/ Reunion:	E	Policy/General Conference:	P

1968-1984: The United Methodist Church--Unity and Diversity

1968: The MC (1939) and the EUBC (1946) unite to form The United Methodist Church (UMC) at Dallas, TX; the Plan of Union eliminates the Central Jurisdiction, but not until 1973 does the last church integate (SC).

1968: A group of EUBC members, primarily in Oregon and Washington, opposed to the merger with the Methodists, withdraws to form the Evangelical Church of North America. Their headquarters is in Minneapolis, MN.

1968: The Wesleyan Methodist Church (1843/1947) and the Pilgrim Holiness Church (1922) merge to form the Wesleyan Church, at Anderson University, Anderson, Indiana.

1970: The CMEC celebrates the centennial of its founding, moves headquarters in Memphis, TN.

1972: A number of important developments emerge from General Conference in Atlanta, Ga:

- General Agencies are consolidated into four "Super-boards":
  General Board of Church and Society (Washington, D.C.)
  General Board of Global Ministries (New York, NY)
  General Board of Discipleship (Nashville, TN)
  General Board of Higher Education & Ministry (Nashville)
  (an older General Board of Pensions, Naperville, IL. existed, while the General Council on Ministries and General Council on Finance and Administration in Nashville TN, have coordinating roles between the General Boards.)

- The Theological Study Commission presents Albert Outler's Wesleyan Quadrilateral to hold together Methodist diversity, placing emphasis on "Method," allowing for latitude in theology.

- Methodist Caucuses Lobby General Conference for the first time; along with Social Principles Study Commission, places social justice squarely in the mainstream of the United Methodist Church.

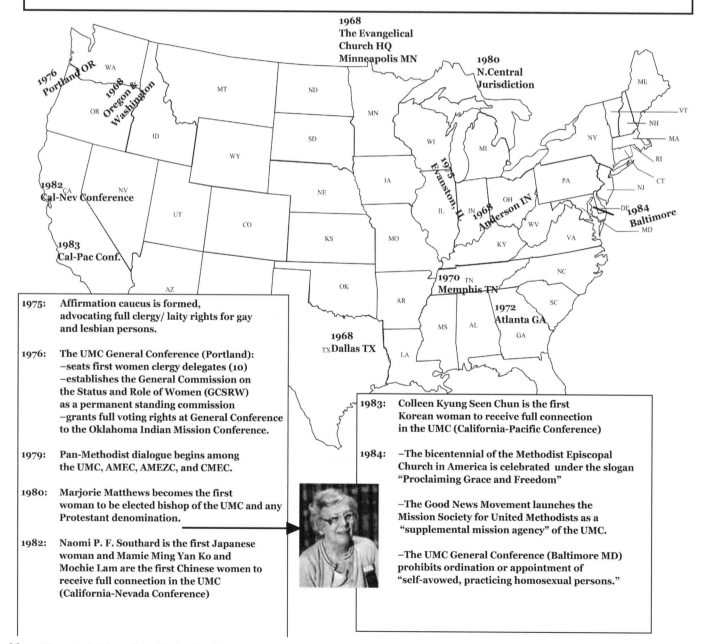

1968 The Evangelical Church HQ Minneapolis MN

1980 N.Central Jurisdiction

1976 Portland OR

1968 Oregon & Washington

1982 Cal-Nev Conference

1983 Cal-Pac Conf.

1975 Evanston, IL

1968 Anderson IN

1984 Baltimore MD

1970 Memphis TN

1972 Atlanta GA

1968 Dallas TX

1975: Affirmation caucus is formed, advocating full clergy/ laity rights for gay and lesbian persons.

1976: The UMC General Conference (Portland):
–seats first women clergy delegates (10)
–establishes the General Commission on the Status and Role of Women (GCSRW) as a permanent standing commission
–grants full voting rights at General Conference to the Oklahoma Indian Mission Conference.

1979: Pan-Methodist dialogue begins among the UMC, AMEC, AMEZC, and CMEC.

1980: Marjorie Matthews becomes the first woman to be elected bishop of the UMC and any Protestant denomination.

1982: Naomi P. F. Southard is the first Japanese woman and Mamie Ming Yan Ko and Mochie Lam are the first Chinese women to receive full connection in the UMC (California-Nevada Conference)

1983: Colleen Kyung Seen Chun is the first Korean woman to receive full connection in the UMC (California-Pacific Conference)

1984: –The bicentennial of the Methodist Episcopal Church in America is celebrated under the slogan "Proclaiming Grace and Freedom"

–The Good News Movement launches the Mission Society for United Methodists as a "supplemental mission agency" of the UMC.

–The UMC General Conference (Baltimore MD) prohibits ordination or appointment of "self-avowed, practicing homosexual persons."

1984: The Affirmation caucus establishes the Reconciling Congregations Program.

1986: The UMC General Board of Global Ministries establishes Korean American missions in all five UMC jurisdictions.

1987: Rose Mary Denman of New Hampshire loses clergy credentials after declaring that she is a lesbian.

1987: "The Houston Declaration" affirms a set of confessional commitments to Scriptural primacy and trinitarian language, as well as support for the UMC ban against the ordination of practicing homosexuality.

1988-1989: Publication of a new UM Hymnal comes under controversy due to gender inclusive language and diverse themes. Once published, it quickly sells.

1992: The Good News Movement issues "The Memphis Declaration," calling on United Methodists "to live more faithfully as the body of Jesus Christ."

1993: Participation by UM women in the first ecumenical feminist Re-Imagining Conference in Minneapolis sparks nationwide controversy.

1995: UMC clergy and laity launch the Confessing Movement for the renewal of The UMC, Atlanta, GA.

1998: The Confessing Movement holds its first annual national conference in Tulsa, OK.

1998: The UMC Judicial Council rules that statements about homosexuality added to the Social Principles in 1996 have church law status.

1998-1999: Jimmy Creech (member of Nebraska Conference) officiates a same-sex union service; he is tried on charges, and loses his credentials.

2001: The UMC Judicial Council rules central conferences outside the U.S. may adapt *The Book of Discipline*, except for matters protected by the UMC constitution.

2003: Bishop Joseph Sprague is tried and acquitted by the North Central Jurisdiction College of Bishops of disseminating doctrines on homosexuality contrary to church law.

2004: Karen Dammann (Pacific Northwest Conference) is acquitted on charges that her admission to being in a committed lesbian relationship constituted practices incompatible with UMC and Christian teaching.

2005: Ed Johnson (Virginia Conference) is suspended by Bishop Charlene Kammerer for refusing church membership to a gay person. He is reinstated after appeal to Judicial Council.

2005: As a "self-avowed, practicing homosexual," Beth Stroud's clergy credentials are stripped by the Judicial Council after lengthy church hearings, appeals, and reversals. She continues to serve as a Pastoral Assistant in an Eastern Pennsylvania Conference local church.

Unity and Diversity in United Methodism:

The pin symbols represent significant tensions which emerged as protest movements, or church litigation, within the five jurisdictions of the UMC.

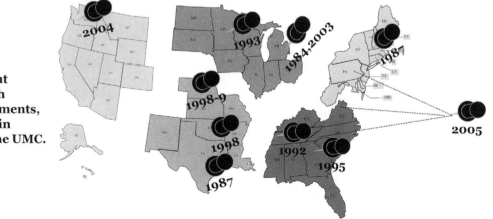

April 2007: The UMC Judicial Council (which litigates appeals of church law based upon American legal models) meets in the Philippines, the first time this Methodist structure has met overseas.

Bibliography

Statistical Sources

Methodist historians (as well as United Brethren, Evangelical Association, AME, and AME Zion) are very fortunate for the early and efficient tendency for leaders to count both "noses and nickels" (membership and financial statistics). Such concerns were traceable back to Wesley's pragmatic need to provide strict accountability in the small classes, in order to further the Wesleyan Revival and corporate sanctification.

For statistics and the spread of the Wesleyan Revival in Great Britain:
Harwood, George H. *The History of Wesleyan Methodism*. London: Whittaker and Co., 1854.

For the statistical development of the Methodist Episcopal Church in America from 1773 to 1860, see:
Goss, Charles Chaucer. *Statistical History of the First Century of American Methodism*. New York: Carlton and Porter, 1866.

For the statistical and narrative development of the Methodist Episcopal Church, South, from 1845 to 1894, see:
Gross, Alexander, *A History of the Methodist Episcopal Church, South, in the United States*. New York: The Christian Literature Company, 1894.

For the statistical and narrative broadening of Methodism as it spread to the Mississippi River, along with good biographical sketches, see:
Bangs, Nathan. *A History of the Methodist Episcopal Church*, 3rd. ed. New York: Published by T. Mason and G. Lane for the Methodist Episcopal Church, 1839–1842.

From 1850 to 1930, the U.S. Census covered religious affiliation, and thus Methodist membership is available at the county level (a level of detail we have chosen not to replicate, see Edwin Gaustad's *Historical Atlas of American Religion* on a decade-by-decade basis). The total membership results can be seen by decade in Abingdon's *The Methodist Experience in America*, Vol. II, up to the year 2000. The United Methodist General Council on Finance and Administration now publishes membership and financial data regularly on their website, including numbers of congregations and pastors, broken down into the various ministry orders and regions.

While mapping the Methodist movement has never been as important as counting its membership gains, American Methodism gave particularly good attention to documenting the date and spread of formal circuits (if not always indicating who was the first Methodist preacher in a given area). Thus the geographic spread of the movement can be traced through circuit rider diaries and conference records of new appointments. Particularly helpful in terms of showing the relationship between geographic centers and margins is the journal of Francis Asbury's travels. Methodist historical geography was fortunately well represented and summarized by Frederick Norwood in *The Story of American Methodism*. This geographic sensitivity and the consolidation of vast amounts of narrative source data on the spread of Methodism—I contend—is one of the hidden reasons for the long shelf life of Norwood's classic text.

Historical Works with Images and Illustrations

Daniels, W.H. *The Illustrated History of Methodism in Great Britain, America, and Australia*. New York: Hunt and Eaton, 1890.

Lednum, John. *A History of the Rise of Methodism in America: Containing Sketches of Methodist Itinerant Preachers, from 1736 to 1785*. Philadelphia: Published by Author, 1859.

Luccock, Naphtali, James Wideman Lee, and James Main Dixon. *The Illustrated History of Methodism: The Story of the Origin and Progress of the Methodist Church, from Its Foundation by John Wesley to the Present Day*. St. Louis and New York: The Methodist Magazine Publishing Co., 1900.

Moore, John Jamison. *History of the A.M.E. Zion Church in America: Founded in 1796, in the City of New York*. York, Pa.: Teachers' Journal Office, 1884.

Primary Historical Sources

Allen, Richard. *The Life, Experience, and Gospel Labours of the Rt. Rev. Richard Allen . . . With an Address to the People of Colour in the United States*. Philadelphia: Published By Allen, Richard, 1833.

Lane, Isaac. *Autobiography of Bishop Isaac Lane, LL.D.: With a Short History of the C.M.E. Church in America and of Methodism*. Nashville: Printed for the author [by] Publishing House of the M.E. Church, South, 1916.

Richey, Russell E., Kenneth E. Rowe, and Jean Miller Schmidt, eds. *The Methodist Experience in America: A Sourcebook*. Nashville: Abingdon Press, 2000.

Tipple, Ezra, ed. *The Heart of Asbury's Journal*. New York: Eaton and Mains, 1904.

Wesley, John. *Journal and Diaries*, 7 vols. (vols. 18–24 in *The Bicentennial Edition of the Works of John Wesley*), eds. W. Reginald Ward and Richard P. Heitzenrater. Nashville: Abingdon Press, 1988.

Secondary Historical Sources

General Surveys

Appleton, D., ed. *Appleton's Annual Encyclopedia 1900*. New York: D. Appleton and Co., 1901.

Breyfogel, Sylvanus Charles. *Landmarks of the Evangelical Association: Containing All the Official Records of the Annual and General Conferences from the Days of Jacob Albright until 1840*. Reading, Pa.: Eagle Book Print, 1888.

Bucke, Emory Stevens, ed. *The History of American Methodism*. 3 vols. Nashville: Abingdon Press, 1964.

Drinkhouse, Edward J. *History of Methodist Reform*. 2 vols. Baltimore: The Board of Publication of the Methodist Protestant Church, 1899.

Hatch, Nathan O. *The Democratization of American Christianity*. New Haven, Conn.: Yale University Press, 1989.

Heitzenrater, Richard P. *Wesley and the People Called Methodists*. Nashville: Abingdon Press, 1995.

Johnson, Charles A. *The Frontier Camp Meeting*. Dallas: Southern Methodist University Press, 1955.

Jones, George Hawkins. *The Methodist Tourist Guidebook Through the Fifty States*. Nashville: Association of Methodist Historical Societies by Tidings, 1966.

Lawrence, John. *History of the United Brethren in Christ*. Vol. I. Dayton, Ohio: United Brethren Printing Establishment, 1868.

Mathews, Donald G. *Religion in the Old South*. Chicago: University of Chicago Press, 1977.

Matthews, Rex D. *Timetables of History for Students of Methodism*. Nashville: Abingdon Press, 2007.

McLeister, Ira F. and Roy S. Nicholson. *Conscience and Commitment: History of the Wesleyan Methodist Church of America*. 4th rev. ed. Marion, Ind.: The Wesley Press, 1976.

Norwood, Frederick A., ed. *Sourcebook of American Methodism*. Nashville: Parthenon Press, 1996. Reprint of the 1983 edition.

———. *The Story of American Methodism: A History of the United Methodists and Their Relations*. Nashville: Abingdon Press, 1974.

Norwood, John Nelson. *The Schism in the Methodist Episcopal Church, 1844: A Study of Slavery and Ecclesiastical Politics*. Alfred, N.Y.: Alfred University Press, 1923.

Potts, J. Manning. "Francis Asbury: The Prophet of the Long Road." *The William and Mary Quarterly*, Second Series, Vol. 22, No. 1 (Jan., 1942): 39–44.

Richey, Russell E. *Early American Methodism*. Bloomington: Indiana University Press, 1991.

Sanford, A.B. *The Methodist Year Book*. New York: Eaton and Mains, 1898.

Schneider, Gregory A. *The Way of the Cross Leads Home: The Domestication of American Methodism*. Bloomington: Indiana University Press, 1993.

Stevens, Abel. *History of the Methodist Episcopal Church in the United States of America, vol. II*. New York: Carlton and Porter, 1864.

Stowell, Jay S. *Methodist Adventures in Negro Education*. New York and Cincinnati: The Methodist Book Concern, 1922.

Sweet, William Warren. *The Methodist Episcopal Church and the Civil War*. Cincinnati: Methodist Book Concern, 1912.

———, ed. *Religion on the American Frontier, 1783-1940: The Methodists, A Collection of Source Materials*. New York: Cooper Square, 1964. Reprint of 1946 edition.

———. "The Rise of Theological Schools in America." *Church History*, Vol. 6, No. 3 (Sep., 1937): 260–73.

Williams, William H. *The Garden of Methodism: The Delmarva Peninsula, 1769–1820*. Wilmington, Del.: Scholarly Resources, 1984.

Yeakel, Reuben. *History of the Evangelical Association, 1750–1850*. Cleveland: Thomas and Mattill, 1895.

Women and Minorities

Gonzalez, Justo L., ed. *Each in Our Own Tongue: A History of Hispanic United Methodism*. Nashville: Abingdon Press, 1991.

Guillermo, Artemio R., ed. *Churches Aflame: Asian Americans and United Methodism*. Nashville: Abingdon Press, 1991.

Noley, Homer. *First White Frost: Native Americans and United Methodism*. Nashville: Abingdon Press, 1991.

Schmidt, Jean Miller. *Grace Sufficient: A History of Women in American Methodism*. Nashville: Abingdon Press, 1999.

Shockley, Grant S., ed. *Heritage and Hope: The African-American Presence in United Methodism*. Nashville: Abingdon Press, 1991.

They Went Out Not Knowing: 100 Women in Mission. New York: General Board of Global Ministries, 1986. electronic version http://gbgm-umc.org/umw/history/.

Mission

Barclay, Wade Crawford. *History of Methodist Missions*. Vol. 1, *Missionary Motivations and Expansion*. New York: The Board of Missions and Church Extension of the Methodist Church, 1949.

———. *History of Methodist Missions*. Vol. 2, *To Reform the Nation*. New York: The Board of Missions and Church Extension of the Methodist Church, 1950.

———. *History of Methodist Missions*. Vol. 3, *Widening Horizons, 1845–1895*. New York: The Board of Missions of the Methodist Church, 1951.

Copplestone, J. Tremayne. *History of Methodist Missions*. Vol. 4, *Twentieth Century Perspectives*. New York: The Board of Global Ministries, The United Methodist Church, 1973.

Ledbetter, Anna and Roma Wyatt. *World Methodist Council. Handbook of Information, 2002–2006*. Revised Edition. Lake Junaluska, N.C.: The World Methodist Council, 2003.

Reference Works

Eltscher, Susan M., ed. *Women in the Wesleyan and United Methodist Traditions: A Bibliography*. Madison, N.J.: General Commission on Archives and History, The United Methodist Church, 1991.

Gray, C. Jarrett, Jr., ed. *The Racial and Ethnic Presence in American Methodism: A Bibliography*. Madison, N.J.: General Commission on Archives and History, The United Methodist Church, 1991.

Harmon, Nolan B., ed. *Encyclopedia of World Methodism*. 2 vols. Nashville: United Methodist Publishing House, 1974.

Waltz, Alan K. *A Dictionary for United Methodists*. Nashville: Abingdon Press, 1991.

Yrigoyen, Jr., Charles, and Susan E. Warrick. *A Historical Dictionary of Methodism,* 2nd edition. Lanham, Md.: Scarecrow Press, 2005.